Praise for

FROM HERE TO SECURITY

A top leader in the field shows where our nation has been and where we need to go to become a nation of savers. Makes a cogent and powerful case for adopting the payroll-based Automatic IRA and expanding workplace saving—automatically enrolling tens of millions of working households in IRAs and employer plans. A concise, engaging, and informative prescription for bipartisan action to give all Americans greater retirement security and a stake in a faster growing economy.

—**J. MARK IWRY,** Nonresident Senior Fellow,
the Brookings Institution, and former Senior
Advisor to the Secretary of the Treasury

It's become fashionable of late to describe the 401(k) plan as a failure. But in his book, Bob Reynolds makes it clear that you can't blame a drought on the well. The 401(k) works fabulously when it's made available to employees by an employer. Unfortunately, too many Americans still do not have access to a 401(k) at work. The many suggestions outlined in the book would go a long toward fixing this problem and allowing Americans the opportunity to achieve a secure retirement. It's not the fault of the 401(k) that not enough people have one. Bob Reynolds has laid out the path to getting there.

—**BRIAN GRAFF,** Chief Executive Officer,
American Retirement Association

Retirement should be something we look forward to, not be worried about, and effective workplace savings programs are critical to ensuring more Americans start saving and can comfortably retire. My friend Bob Reynolds has a passion for addressing our retirement challenges, and has spent decades helping millions of Americans achieve a secure retirement. I worked closely with him on the Portman-Cardin reforms that expanded retirement savings, and I continue to seek his counsel today. This new book examines America's retirement system honestly and comprehensively, and makes the case that further strengthening defined contribution retirement plans offers us a way to increase savings, and gives more Americans the peace of mind that comes with having a secure retirement.

—**ROB PORTMAN,** Senior Senator from Ohio and
Member of the Senate Committee on Finance

An edifying, pragmatic, and important contribution to the retirement security debate. This clear-eyed analysis of where we've been and where we're going should be required reading for policy makers, business executives, and nonprofit leaders—or anyone interested in helping Americans retire with dignity. The bold ideas in this volume—especially proposals for national automatic IRAs, refundable tax credits for retirement savings, and "birthright retirement accounts"—would, if enacted, be a huge step forward in our quest to build an inclusive savings system that builds financial security for all.

—**IDA RADEMACHER,** Director, The Aspen
Institute's Financial Security Initiative

Bob Reynolds is a true leader on retirement policy and an outspoken supporter for providing workplace savings to all Americans. For years, he's promoted innovative solutions to addressing our retirement crisis, including his continued support for my proposal, the automatic IRA, which would provide a retirement savings opportunity at work for millions of workers that's in addition to Social Security. I applaud Bob for his relentless drive to ensure that all Americans are financially secure in retirement.

—**CONGRESSMAN RICHARD E. NEAL,**
Ranking Member House Ways and Means Committee

America has an urgent need to get more people better prepared for retirement. Bob Reynolds answers the call by clearly and boldly outlining his ideas to help solve the challenges workers and families across America face as they struggle to save for retirement.

—**GOVERNOR TIM PAWLENTY,** CEO and President,
Financial Services Roundtable

Retirement security is an essential but often overlooked driver of economic growth. When individuals are given the tools to save for retirement, they're not only securing their futures, they're fueling the capital markets that drive our economy. As one of the pioneers of workplace retirement savings, Bob Reynolds has dedicated his career to giving consumers those tools and strengthening the economy for all of us. In *From Here to Security* he applies his trademark passion and pragmatism to a public policy challenge that is highly technical, deeply personal, and unquestionably consequential for our nation's future.

—**TOM DONOHUE,** President and CEO,
U.S. Chamber of Commerce

The economics of retirement combine complicated policy questions about finance with complex cultural questions about personal responsibility. Few leaders from any sector can rival the deep expertise that Robert Reynolds brings to bear on these challenging issues. Any reader who cares about the future of the U.S. economy should dig into *From Here to Security* and learn from his hard-won experience.

—**ARTHUR BROOKS**, President,
American Enterprise Institute

Retirement savings are not just about helping secure income for retirees. They are a critical component of our whole economy. They fuel America's world-leading capital markets and help millions of working families create real wealth. For decades, Bob Reynolds has spoken out for public policies to increase retirement savings and help all working Americans gain access to savings plans on the job. I've had the pleasure of working with Bob on ways to simplify our tax code and ensure that retirement savings are protected and expanded. Because as he points out in this vital book, stronger retirement savings can actually help drive faster growth—our top national goal. *From Here to Security* lays out clear, practical ways to achieve that.

—**CONGRESSMAN KEVIN P. BRADY**,
Chairman, House Ways & Means Committee

From Here to Security offers unique insights on how to shape the future of American retirement that every plan sponsor, participant, retiree, and policy maker should embrace. Based upon Reynolds's decades of continuous experimentation and testing, he sets forth a game plan for the nation to move from the 50-yard line to the goal line for the touchdown of retirement security.

—**DALLAS L. SALISBURY**, Resident Fellow and
President Emeritus, Employee Benefit Research Institute

Saving is vital to any country's economic health. For households, it builds resilience against life events and creates wealth that can ensure an adequate income in retirement. For any nation, saving provides a vital engine for long-term economic prosperity and stability. Bob Reynolds is to be congratulated on his compelling analysis of these benefits and for highlighting the critical role of workplace plans in encouraging people to save.

—**ADRIAN COOPER**, CEO, Oxford Economics

Ensuring that all Americans can retire with dignity is an ongoing and ever-evolving policy effort. Drawing on his impressive experience in the retirement savings space, Bob Reynolds provides a thorough accounting of the many retirement challenges facing workers and families, along with thoughtful proposals on improving access, increasing savings, and converting those savings into lifetime income. Mr. Reynolds's book makes the compelling case that retirement security is truly a bipartisan goal worth fighting for—and a goal that has not only powerful economic consequences, but also immense psychological, political, and social value.

> —**BEN CARDIN,** Senior Senator from Maryland
> and member of the Senate Committee on Finance

Retirement deficits for all U.S. households currently ages 35–64 are simulated to be $4.13 trillion according to EBRI's Retirement Security Projection Model.* It was clear that a bold plan is needed to both improve the level of deficit reduction overall and focus specifically on those who had already reached age 55. The plan that Bob Reynolds describes in this book is indeed such a plan. If adopted, the Empower Retirement Workplace 4.0 agenda for reforms would make a larger "dent" in America's savings shortfall than any retirement reform proposal EBRI has analyzed. Some shortfalls would remain, notably among the very poor and among those who require costly long-term nursing home care. These challenges are not easily met through workplace savings alone. But the proposals offered in Bob Reynolds's book would be a *huge* step forward for working Americans and for our economy.

> —**JACK VANDERHEI,** Director of Research,
> the Employee Benefit Research Institute (EBRI)

Retirement security is one of many great and growing challenges we face today. In meeting these challenges, we are all better off when Bob Reynolds brings his voice to the public square. His insight on the public debate helps facilitate the solution-oriented thinking we need.

> —**CONGRESSMAN PETER J. ROSKAM,** Chairman,
> Tax Policy Subcommittee, House Ways and Means Committee

FROM HERE

HOW WORKPLACE SAVINGS CAN

TO SECURITY

KEEP AMERICA'S PROMISE

ROBERT L. REYNOLDS

WITH

LENNY GLYNN AND JOHN MITCHEM

Mc Graw Hill Education

New York   Chicago   San Francisco   Athens   London   Madrid
Mexico City   Milan   New Delhi   Singapore   Sydney   Toronto

1 2 3 4 5 6 7 8 9   LCR   22 21 20 19 18 17

ISBN   978-1-260-11607-6
MHID   1-260-11607-7

e-ISBN   978-1-260-11608-3
e-MHID   1-260-11608-5

McGraw-Hill Education books are available at special quantity discounts to use as
premiums and sales promotions or for use in corporate training programs. To contact
a representative, please visit the Contact Us pages at www.mhprofessional.com.

_Dedicated to the working people of America
who deserve financial freedom and dignity
in retirement, and to my parents, Bill and
Juanita Reynolds, with limitless thanks._

Find the good and praise it.
—**ALEX HALEY**, author, *Roots*

*When considering any major policy change,
it is essential, not optional, to weigh the
political feasibility, not just the design
elegance, of any proposed solution.*
—**RICHARD PARKER**, author,
*John Kenneth Galbraith:
His Life, His Politics, His Economics*

*To see what is in front of one's nose
needs a constant struggle.*
—**GEORGE ORWELL**

CONTENTS

ACKNOWLEDGMENTS

The fact that I've dedicated this book to my parents suggests, rightly, that I owe debts of gratitude that go back decades—to those who've shaped my views and made this book possible. So thanks to my great professors and fellow students at West Virginia University, who gave me my first insights into finance. Thanks to dozens of people I worked with at Fidelity Investments—too many to name—who made it possible for us to build America's largest retirement services firm. And special thanks to Edward "Ned" Johnson, an amazing business genius, who asked me to take on the challenge of creating a new company, FIRSCo, to serve a then-small market—called "401(k)"—back in 1988. Working for Ned Johnson was a real privilege.

Thanks, too, to all those who helped prepare this text. First, to Lenny Glynn, who has worked with me on policy and speechwriting since the turn of this new millennium, and whose deft hand is visible throughout; to our collaborator, John Mitchem, whose research helped deepen our database and widen our global scope; to Sue Asci and Rene Taber, whose fact-checking and permission-securing was essential; to Dan Kennedy and his design team at Putnam who developed our cover concept; to Boston's best PowerPoint maven, Steve Madero; and to the two best aides any CEO could have: Susan Talmage and Melinda Costanzo. Thanks to our savvy editor at McGraw Hill, Donya Dickerson. Let me also propose a toast to John "Ike" Williams, our deservedly legendary lawyer/agent/counselor—and pal.

Kudos to the men and women like Jack VanDerhei, Dallas Salisbury, Mark Iwry, Merl Baker, Bridget Madrian, Richard Thaler, and many others—who devote their professional and academic lives to the retirement research that we've drawn on so heavily. And a great shout-out to farsighted political leaders like Senators Rob Portman and Ben Cardin and Congressman Richie Neal—who use those insights to craft legislation that has improved the lives of millions of working Americans. Most of all, thanks to my awe-inspiring wife, Laura, to my children, and to all young Americans: lifting up your futures inspired us to raise this call for change.

May you all go . . . From Here to Security.

PREFACE

I didn't plan on this when I was growing up, but building retirement security in America has turned out to be my life's mission.

From leading the 401(k) business at Fidelity Investments in the 1980s, to becoming CEO at Putnam Investments in 2008, to helping create America's second-largest retirement services firm, Empower Retirement, in 2014, I've spent more than three decades working to grow and continuously improve America's workplace savings system.

Over 30 years ago, I was there for the infancy of the 401(k). I've seen multiple generations of change in workplace savings since then, as 401(k)s and other defined contribution (DC) plans expanded, evolved, and matured to become Americans' primary source of future retirement income.

I've had a hands-on, close-up view of the dynamic changes in workplace savings, such as digital reporting, web-based planning tools, and target date funds that align with a saver's planned retirement date. Some of these changes, like steadily falling fees, were driven largely by market competition. Some stemmed from insights in behavioral finance, some from wise public policy, notably the Pension Protection Act of 2006, which was the first time Congress seriously treated DC plans as a central element of America's retirement picture. Over all these years, I've seen amazing progress toward a most worthy goal: the chance for a dignified retirement for all.

But the job is not done. We still have miles to go to bring all working Americans from here to retirement security.

This book aims to show the way. I believe—and I hope to convince you—that we can solve America's retirement challenge, just as we solved the challenge of polio, or getting to the moon, or creating the Internet. Better still, by doing so, Americans can begin to restore our faith in our ability to govern ourselves. And best of all, by increasing our savings rate and channeling those savings to capital markets, we can help America's economy to grow far more robustly.

We have a great base of public and private retirement systems to build on. Our workplace savings—401(k) plans and similar payroll deduction options—already provide a vital supplement to Social Security. Together, Social Security and workplace savings blend common purpose and individual aspiration in ways that strengthen both.

Think of it this way: Social Security is an obligation that working Americans owe to each other across the generations; workplace savings is a voluntary opportunity that each of us owes to ourselves and to our families.

Given its central role in reducing the once-routine tragedy of elderly poverty, Social Security may well be America's greatest public policy achievement of the twentieth century. It provides a life-and-death income source for low-income retirees. It is critical for middle- and upper-middle-income retirees as well. And, as we will see, it offers a serious share of income—even to the affluent, well up into the top tenth of Americans by wealth.

Both the public retirement finance system, Social Security, and the private system of workplace savings need strengthening, and the ways to do that are quite straightforward.

I say that with some confidence because the rise of workplace savings plans over the past generation, especially since the

Pension Protection Act of 2006, constitutes a massive socio-economic experiment conducted right in plain sight. And the results are in. We can clearly see how crucial Social Security is as a baseline. And we can see how retirement plan design, technology, professional guidance, and individual savings behavior combine to deliver on the most basic goal: reliably replacing preretirement income for life. That metric—retirement readiness—is what all savings systems aim to achieve.

And based on what we see in the comprehensive Lifetime Income Surveys (LIS) we do at Empower Retirement, and previously at Putnam Investments, I would argue that the three core solutions to America's retirement savings challenge are blindingly obvious: (1) make Social Security solvent, (2) extend workplace savings options to all working Americans, and (3) make all workplace savings plans fully automatic and aim for savings of 10 percent or more. Challenge met. Problem solved.

But as George Orwell shrewdly noted, "To see what is in front of one's nose needs a constant struggle." And when it comes to retirement policy, that struggle is almost entirely political.

Being political, debate on retirement issues is often marred by one-dimensional analyses, ideological biases, and sheer hype. We see a constant flood of books and articles pitching the idea of a looming retirement "crisis." Putting forward such frightening predictions has become a cottage industry. Anxiety, fear, and blame may sell, but these fear-mongering books and articles grossly exaggerate the real challenges we face.

Many critics use unfair, one-sided, and partial analyses to argue that we're heading for a retirement finance abyss or that the 401(k) system is somehow a failure. They go on from those false premises to propose radical changes that have no chance of ever happening, such as scrapping 401(k)s in favor of a new government-run savings model. Such proposals strike me as exercises in futility. None of these schemes for total overhaul make real politically feasible reform any easier.

My view is that, despite multiple imperfections, Social Security and our evolving system of workplace savings actually complement each other's strengths. Without conscious planning, we in America have evolved a hybrid retirement finance engine that enables workers to benefit from diversified income sources, drawing on both labor (through Social Security taxes) and capital (from investment returns to workplace savings). And despite some serious flaws, this hybrid system simply needs strengthening, not radical reworking.

We don't need to create any major new systems or institutions. Social Security does need to be made solvent—and that's a major challenge for politicians—but it doesn't need to be reinvented. As for workplace savings, I say—with a hat-tip to Bill Clinton's famous comment about America itself—"There's nothing wrong with the 401(k) that can't be fixed by what's right about the 401(k)."

America's workplace savings plans have already helped more than 80 million workers accumulate more than $7 trillion in their job-based retirement accounts and another $8 trillion in Individual Retirement Accounts (IRAs). (Most of the money in IRAs has, in fact, "rolled over" from job-based savings plans.) This vast pool of savings is one of the greatest success stories in financial history. It is the envy of nations around the world, few of which have anything like it.

Fully funded workplace savings give the United States a huge competitive advantage over nations whose pay-as-you-go retirement systems are funded only notionally, by politicians' promises and cash flows from taxes on current workers' wages. Such pay-as-you-go retirement systems often appear generous, but as populations age, they are proving unsustainable and crisis-prone, driving social unrest, fiscal crises, and threats of national default.

By contrast, Americans' fully funded defined contribution savings plans both fuel and benefit from the world's deepest, most liquid capital markets for stocks, bonds, and other securities. They stabilize the economy in downturns by enabling retirees to sustain their lifestyles and continue to consume. More important, workplace savings have democratized investing in America. Tens of millions of working Americans can look forward to living in retirement on income from dividends, interest, and capital gains.

We often forget how great an achievement this actually is. For most of human history, even in America, capital income was the exclusive privilege of a wealthy few. Today, our workplace savings plans are well along in creating a people's capitalism that can, and should, give ownership and equity to all.

Yet, as I mentioned, far too many books and commentar ies about workplace savings and retirement policy in America speak of "crisis" or "failure." Their authors zone in on short-falls and flaws in the system. They focus obsessively on alleged unfairness in the way savings benefits are distributed. They call for radical reforms and whole new institutions to replace a supposedly broken, irredeemable status quo.

In response, retirement services industry spokespeople and trade groups often issue monograph-length white papers, books, and reports that focus only on the strengths that I mentioned.

These would-be defenders insist that our retirement savings systems are doing quite well, with little need for change.

I take a very different approach.

I do recognize the shortcomings of America's retirement systems, both public and private. They are real and serious. I have seen them up close. I have tried over many years to get them corrected. I know that these problems are not fabricated by the system's critics. But I also know they are eminently fixable. And I favor a practical, fruitful, effective way to go about fixing anything—including retirement savings. Alex Haley, the author of *Roots*, had this approach to positive change: "Find the good and praise it." It has near-universal application.

So when it comes to retirement policy, the best way to start toward serious progress is to look honestly at what's working well. The next step is to find ways to spread these proven best practices and structures to serve as many people as possible. Focus on what's working. Aim to make success contagious. That approach, I believe, offers far better chances of real progress than focusing only on shortfalls and flaws. What we need are practical, incremental improvements to existing structures and institutions—not fantasies that will never pass Congress.

Imagining perfect solutions that would require massive, politically impossible change is a natural temptation. "Big" ideas are often more exciting and dramatic than small changes. But in retirement policy, as in most areas of debate, the perfect can very often be the enemy of the good.

I am proposing steady positive changes to existing systems, especially the workplace savings that most Americans already enjoy. I believe the data from our huge experiment in workplace savings already tells us what's working, and what we need to do to fix what's not working. Like a doctor who has discovered a vaccine that can cure a serious disease, I feel a moral obligation to spread the word about reforms and best practices that can inoculate our country against the risk of a very predictable rise in elderly poverty.

I aim to speak to the people who can actually make positive change happen in the retirement world: well-informed citizens, business owners, trade associations and labor union leaders, policy makers in the House and Senate, CEOs, entrepreneurs, and heads of human resources and benefits departments, as well as journalists and scholars who cover retirement and economic issues.

I will show specific ways our workplace savings systems can be improved on, often just by getting behind and supporting positive initiatives that are already underway. But make no mistake: These small changes would compound into huge, qualitative improvements for tens of millions of working people. Taken together, they can combine to significantly lift savings rates in America, dramatically improve all working Americans' chances of achieving retirement security, and spur our economy into a higher gear.

These are high stakes—and positive stakes—to play for.

To understand why action to lift Americans' saving rate is so needed, we have to begin with a look at just how seriously American retirement savings and policy are falling short today.

CHAPTER 1

AMERICA'S RETIREMENT SAVINGS CHALLENGE

The only thing we have to fear is fear itself.
—**FRANKLIN D. ROOSEVELT**, Inaugural Address, 1933

America's retirement future can certainly seem terribly threatening. In every media outlet—from books to blogs, TV to Twitter, magazines to think-tank white papers and academic studies, a host of troubling reports suggest that we're on the cusp of a pervasive retirement "crisis." They warn of a coming wave of elderly poverty and bitter intergenerational conflicts that pit America's boomers against millennials, their own children.

These grim scenarios are exaggerated. But they are not wholly groundless. America's retirement savings challenge is very real. Here are some points to consider:

- About two-thirds of private sector workers have access to any kind of employer-sponsored retirement savings plan, according to the Pew Research Center.

- 52 percent of Americans are at risk of a substantially reduced standard of living in retirement, according to Boston College's most recent National Retirement Risk Index.
- U.S. households headed by men and women between the ages of 25 and 64 face an aggregate retirement savings deficit of some $4 trillion, according to the Employee Benefit Research Institute (EBRI).
- Only about 50 percent of American workers between the ages of 25 and 64 actually take part in employer-sponsored retirement plans, whether defined benefit or defined contribution.
- A typical U.S. household retires with only $111,000 in 401(k) or IRA savings, in addition to any traditional pension, Social Security, or nonretirement assets (notably private business assets or real estate) they may own.
- Roughly one-third of American households have zero retirement savings and will be forced to rely on Social Security as their only financial resource in retirement, according to Social Security's own database.
- 46 percent of American households cannot come up with $400 cash for an emergency without borrowing from credit cards, friends, or family, according to a recent survey by the Federal Reserve.
- Roughly 46 percent of senior citizens in America die with less than $10,000 to their names, according to a 2012 study for the National Bureau of Economic Research (NBER). The "oldest elders," those in their late eighties, nineties, and beyond, are often totally destitute.
- Empower Retirement's own annual Lifetime Income Survey (LIS), developed in collaboration with Brightwork Partners, finds that, at the median, working Americans are

2

on track to replace only 62 percent of their previous income once they stop working.

The LIS is one of the most comprehensive analyses of retirement income prospects. It includes virtually all sources of potential retirement income, from all forms of retirement savings, plus Social Security, home equity, and business ownership. Its overall finding, that Americans can replace just 62 percent of their pre-retirement income at the median, suggests that many millions of future retirees will have to dial back their spending significantly once they stop working, or face severe financial stress.

All of these findings, and others like them, tell us that Americans' savings are too low and that the threat of future distress is too serious to ignore. But averages and system-wide data don't necessarily tell the whole story. Nor do they point to useful strategies for action. To find potential solutions, we need to dig below the headlines and draw vital distinctions between the categories of workers, types of savings plans, and plan designs that generate vastly different retirement outcomes. When we do, a much more nuanced picture emerges, a mosaic of widely varying levels of retirement readiness.

At the upper end of the retirement readiness scale are millions of workers in large and midsize companies who are well on their way to successful retirements. They will be able to replace close to, or even more than, 100 percent of the income they earned while working. These workers are typically, but not exclusively, above average in income. But what drives their success is not higher income *per se*, but the fact that they have access to, and take full advantage of, well-designed, largely automated payroll savings plans on the job.

Just below these highly successful savers is a retirement-readiness middle ground of workers who also have access to workplace savings plans but whose plans may lack some of the most effective automatic design features. Some of these midrange workers may also not fully engage with their plans or not maximize their savings. Many face competing financial demands, such as housing costs or student loans. Others simply choose to save less and spend more.

At the low end of the income scale are tens of millions of workers who lack access to any form of payroll deduction plan on the job. Too many low- to moderate-income employees in small companies simply have no payroll deduction savings options. Millions more self-employed workers, part-timers, or those involved in contingent labor or the "gig economy" are also outside the tent when it comes to retirement savings.

For these Americans, Social Security will provide the vast majority of retirement income. And the good news is that the system can provide enough income replacement to help workers of modest means avoid outright poverty. But we can, and should, do much more than that baseline minimum.

We can clearly see that America's payroll deduction retirement system already has the potential to deliver successful retirement outcomes because it is actually doing that for millions of households today. And this made-in-America system of defined contribution savings plans is fully funded and economically sustainable, unlike many seemingly more generous public retirement systems around the world.

But however successful America's workplace savings system is at its best, that success is only partial. Millions of American workers remain outside this exercise in mass investing and wealth creation. They have little or no ownership stake in free enterprise capitalism.

Having dedicated much of my career to building the American defined contribution retirement industry, that raw fact makes me impatient, even angry. Bringing these fellow Americans into our workplace savings system strikes me simply as the right thing to do, morally and economically.

It is also time to recognize that most of the shortfalls and flaws we worry about in America's retirement picture don't stem from the structure of 401(k) plans or from the decline of defined benefit pensions, or any other element of retirement policy. Retirement savings shortfalls are often driven by deep long-term trends, most of which are far more powerful than any aspect of workplace plan design or retirement policy itself.

The Chain of Causality

To understand why we face a retirement shortfall, we need to consider forces and trends that have cut across the U.S. economy for decades. Retirement is, let's recall, the time when a host of economic and cultural forces that have been at work for decades combine to deliver economic and financial outcomes to members of a generation at the end of their working lives.

Thus, retired Americans now in their late nineties have been touched by events as distant as the Great Depression, World War II, and, over decades, the evolution of safety net programs like Social Security and Medicare. By contrast, boomers, now on the cusp of retirement, likely take those safety net programs for granted. But their financial lives have almost surely been meaningfully benefited by the long stock market boom from 1982 to 2000, and then hurt in mid-to-late career by the stock and housing market crashes of 2000 and 2008–2009. Millennials, those born between 1982 and 2004, also lived through two market slumps, the dot.com crash of 2000 and the far more severe Great Recession of 2008–2009. These experiences, along with the market recovery since 2009, have surely shaped their retirement savings behavior.

Among the multiple factors accounting for America's retirement finance challenge today is a world-historic shift in longevity plus growing disparities in education, health, work, wages, and wealth, and even family structure.

Demographics

By far the most powerful driver of our retirement savings challenge is life itself, specifically the global longevity revolution that we are in the midst of right now.

Every element of America's retirement system, along with retirement systems in every country on this planet, is being stressed by global aging. This historically unprecedented, massive, and glacially powerful force is transforming nations' finances, economics, politics, culture, and future growth prospects. The graying of humanity is a daunting, but actually wonderful, problem that has happened in a historical heartbeat.

Over the course of a typical baby boomer's lifetime, from 1950 to 2025, global human life expectancy is on track to increase by 50 percent, from 48 to 73 years. For the United

States and other developed nations, the increase in longevity beyond age 70 will be greater still.

Longer and healthier lives are arguably the most positive socioeconomic development in all of human history. Economic development, nutrition, quality healthcare, new technologies, and better lifestyle choices have created a perfect storm, delivering an extraordinary extension of human life expectancy despite the wars, terrorism, AIDS, and other horrors reported by the media on a daily basis. The prospect of longer life, I have to say, is the ultimate in good news.

But this good fortune comes with a cost, most obviously in the demands that it places on retirement finance systems. Most of these systems, like Social Security, were established decades ago and designed to support people who then lived on average only into their early or mid seventies.

These systems are poorly suited to serve a new generation of elders whose average life expectancy at age 65 will rise by nearly four full years from 81 to 85—a gain of roughly 25 percent—between 1980 and 2020 (Figure 1.1). And since that's just an average, we'll see millions of these retirees live well into their nineties and beyond. Based on current trends, this remarkable life extension, and the financial stress it creates, will continue for decades.

This historic change poses a very specific business challenge. When I began my career in the 1980s, the average retirement lasted roughly 16 years. Now we need to help people save for, and finance, a retirement that may average 25 percent longer and run 25 to 30 years or more. Financing that long a "vacation" is no easy task.

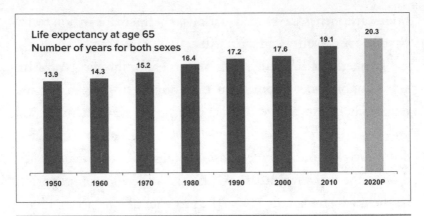

FIGURE 1.1 Americans have added 5 years to their life expectancy at age 65 since 1950

Source: Centers for Disease Control and Prevention (data based on death certificates), 2020 Projection from National Center for Health Statistics, "An Unhealthy America: Economic Burden of Chronic Disease" (2007), Milken Institute.

The longevity revolution is a perfect example of what economists call systemic stress. Longevity takes its toll on all of America's retirement systems: Social Security, traditional pensions, and the emerging defined contribution pension system.

But longer life is not the only thing that's making successful retirement savings tougher. Rising education and healthcare costs, stagnant wages, and profound changes in family structure all compound the challenge.

Education Costs

Education, particularly postsecondary university education, has become vastly more costly for all Americans. Over the past 30 years, a typical family income has increased by 147 percent and the Consumer Price Index (CPI) has increased by 115 percent. But the cost of postsecondary education soared by 500 percent. For parents, the cost of providing for their children's education can conflict directly with their own goal of compiling a retirement savings nest egg.

Students, too, face a financially draining explosion of debt. Today, some 44 million Americans owe more than $1.3 trillion in student loans. Some carry student debt for much of their adult life, and a few all the way into retirement. At any given time, nearly half of these loans are delinquent or in deferment, forbearance, or default.

Student loans make it much harder for young workers to get started early on retirement savings. This delay, in turn, deprives young workers of the single most powerful factor that makes for a successful retirement strategy: the *time* for their investment returns to compound.

Healthcare

Healthcare costs negatively affect retirement savings in the same way as education costs and debt. They divert funds that could be socked away in a 401(k), IRA, or similar savings vehicle. During retirement, out-of-pocket expenses not covered by Medicare can eat up income and even erode principal. And healthcare costs have been outpacing inflation and wages for many years. According to the U.S. Federal Reserve, the CPI has risen by some 235 percent since 1980, while the Consumer Price Index for Medical Care rose by 441 percent (Figure 1.2).

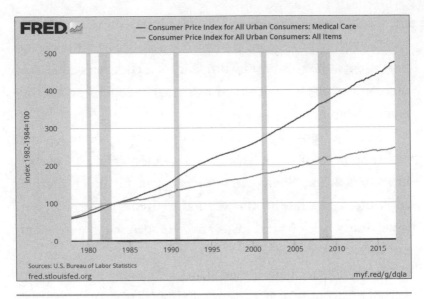

FIGURE 1.2   Consumer Price Index for medical care versus all items

Source: U.S. Bureau of Labor Statistics and Federal Reserve.

Wage Stagnation

But inflation-adjusted real wages for most U.S. workers have scarcely budged since the 1980s. This is problematic since both Social Security benefits and private retirement savings are funded by payroll deductions.

In the three decades after the Second World War, hourly compensation roughly tracked productivity. But over the past 30 to 40 years, productivity has massively outstripped wages, resulting in boom times for capital investment against a backdrop of stagnant wages.

The culprits are well known: globalization, offshoring of industrial jobs, automation of manufacturing processes, dwindling union membership, and the expanding role of less labor-intensive knowledge industries like finance, technology, healthcare, and professional services.

Most of these fast-growing job categories rely on defined contribution retirement savings as their primary retirement vehicle, as compared with government employment or private firms in mature industrial sectors, where most remaining defined benefit plans are found.

As the economy has shifted toward services and knowledge-based industries, employment markets have grown more volatile, with companies staffing up amid growth and then rapidly downsizing, even during mild recessions and stock market dislocations.

Economists appreciate the fact that the United States has a fast-changing, dynamic economy. But this job market volatility, together with the rise of defined contribution workplace savings, directly exposes workers to both a roller-coaster employment market and investment market risk as asset prices move up and down with greater frequency.

Increased personal risk, flat wage growth, and weaker collective bargaining combine to foster a generalized feeling of insecurity among wage earners. This makes many workers reluctant to engage with retirement savings, unless they work for companies that automatically enroll them in payroll savings plans.

Market Shocks

The two major stock market downturns since the beginning of the new millennium have also weakened many Americans' retirement readiness. As always, there is a painful asymmetry between market losses and recovery: you need a 100 percent rebound to recover from a 50 percent loss, plus the ability to be patient and keep a cool head.

Most 401(k) investors did manage to ride out both the popping of the dot.com bubble in 2000 and the far more serious global financial crisis of 2008–2009. Far from selling out at market bottoms, most American workplace savers continued to make their regular 401(k) contributions, paycheck by paycheck, right through those unnerving market slumps. This steady flow of investment effectively raised their equity stakes while stocks were deeply discounted, thus rebuilding their retirement nest eggs.

But some K-plan participants *did* sell low and lock in unrecoverable losses. And some retirees who didn't panic nevertheless found that they had no choice but to sell assets even as markets were falling because they needed to draw income to live on. No one who experienced any such "sequence of returns" risk—having to sell into a declining market—will find much comfort in knowing that markets later rebounded.

Even though the damage that these twin market dips inflicted was limited, not catastrophic, the unprecedented monetary policy responses that followed the 2008–2009 slump are inflicting fresh pain, especially on very conservative retirement savers who rely on bond or bank interest to get by.

Policy Aftershocks

In particular, the zero interest rate policy (ZIRP) of the Federal Reserve and other central banks worldwide, which drove interest rates down in the hope of spurring economic recovery, has made it far more difficult for individual investors to find safe and reliable sources of interest income. Interest rates had already been in secular decline in the United States for over 30 years, which helped fuel the long stock market boom from 1982 to 2000. But the Fed's multiyear limbo dance since 2008— down to near-zero interest rates—is historically unprecedented and potentially dangerous.

For people who are still busy building wealth, ultra-low rates deliver a sharp prod to reach for riskier, more volatile investments in search of higher yield. This accounts in part for the stock market rally we've seen since 2009. But for those already retired and drawing down wealth, ultra-low rates slash the income generated by high-grade bonds, annuities, and other low-risk products. This can further dissuade retirees from buying guaranteed lifetime income products and increase the risk that they will outlive their savings.

Ultra-low rates also wreak havoc on the liability-matching strategies most defined benefit plans use to meet their future obligations. With each passing year of these rock-bottom interest rates, the central banks of the world are relentlessly squeezing pension fund managers everywhere, hastening the decline of defined benefit plans in America and raising the risk of pension failures worldwide.

The Social Fabric

Another trend that is hampering Americans' ability to save for retirement comes from social trends that are well beyond the realm of economics.

The rising incidence of single-person households has very clear and damaging financial impacts. Any financial planner will tell you that divorce, affecting roughly half of marriages, can be a catastrophic financial event for those involved. The savings and home equity of a single household are generally divided between the couple, while living expenses surge for a divided household.

One piece of good news is that America's divorce rate, after rising for generations, has turned down in recent years. But in this case, the "data behind the data" is not comforting. Divorce rates are falling simply because more Americans don't marry in the first place, or they don't remarry or otherwise form couples. Whatever the reason, we are seeing more single heads of household, and this fragmentation of traditional family structures weakens a traditional financial support system and makes retirement savings more difficult.

An even more nuanced take on the structure of our households is that, over the generations, we have developed a marked class divide when it comes to married partners—what sociologists call "associative mating." Whereas a generation or two ago, educated men or women might marry less educated partners, today highly educated, high-earning men and women tend to marry each other. Lower-earning couples do likewise, thereby compounding the inequality of earnings, wealth, and retirement preparation.

A Challenge, Not a Crisis

As we consider ways to improve retirement savings, let's first recognize that many of the deficits in our retirement preparation have much more to do with the changing nature of America's economy and our society than they do with workplace savings plan design. The shift to 401(k)s and similar defined contribution savings has not caused rising healthcare or education costs or the changes we see in family structure.

Today's very real sense of retirement insecurity is *not* the fault of the retirement industry or of changes in workplace plan design. It reflects the culmination of multiple trends that get conflated with retirement issues simply because, let's face it, retirement is the last stop on life's timeline.

The evolution of our retirement structure, from traditional defined benefit pensions to workplace savings plans, has taken place alongside a cascading transformation of our whole economy and American society. Too often, critics of our retirement savings systems are confusing coincidence with causality.

Some of these critics wish nostalgically for a return to traditional defined benefit pensions. They ignore the fact that such pensions never covered more than one-third of long-term workers—"lifers"—and then, mainly at large companies and government agencies. Today, no corporation or government agency is inclined to initiate, expand, or prolong defined benefit pensions; that's the reality we must face.

More positively, as we will see, a wide range of research and industry data make it clear that well-structured defined contribution workplace savings plans can successfully deliver reliable lifetime income in retirement.

Despite its manifold imperfections, our retirement finance architecture today is as well funded as it has ever been in our history. In fact, the United States is uniquely positioned among major industrial nations. We have retirement finance systems in place that massively support both capital formation and social welfare. And because we have both a younger demographic and far more robust private retirement savings, America's retirement system will prove more sustainable over the coming decades than many seemingly more generous systems in other countries.

So, yes, America does face a serious retirement savings challenge. But we don't face any insoluble or overwhelming "crisis." America's retirement services industry has already identified a full tool kit of measures to meet the challenge, ranging from industry best practices that can be spread much more widely, to new public policies that complement and help support private initiatives. So while we do have a tough job ahead, we also have the insights, tools, and techniques that can dramatically improve our workplace savings system and see that it delivers on its full potential.

Before I discuss those changes, though, let me emphasize the urgency of restoring the critical foundation of our entire retirement system: Social Security. Making Social Security solvent for generations to come is, absolutely, job number one in American retirement policy.

RETIREMENT'S BEDROCK: SOCIAL SECURITY

All we want are the facts, Ma'am.
—JACK WEBB as Joe Friday in the 1950s
police drama *Dragnet*

Everyone is entitled to their own opinion.
But they are not entitled to their own facts.
—SENATOR DANIEL PATRICK MOYNIHAN

Apart from ensuring national security and domestic tranquility, the most vital goal for the president and Congress should be rebuilding Americans' shaken belief that their government can actually work for the people; their loss of faith that government can work for them is deeply corrosive to our future. And no domestic policy achievement could do more to recapture lost trust than action to save our Social Security system, the country's largest, most successful, and most popular government program.

Simply put, the system is a life-and-death resource for low- and moderate-income seniors and for millions of disabled people and survivors. It is vital in keeping middle-class retirees' heads above water. And Social Security income is surprisingly important even for those well in the top 10 percent of retirees by wealth. (See box, "Social Security for the Well-to-Do," later in this chapter.) Indeed, the system has become a central pillar of almost *all* Americans' retirement income.

Its most striking success is one that all Americans can be proud of: helping to cut the incidence of poverty among elders from 35 percent of seniors in 1959 to just 10 percent today, actually lifting America's elderly into better financial shape than the young. Fully 60 percent of retirees now receive the majority of their incomes from the system; 21 percent of married couples and 43 percent of unmarried elders depend on it for over 90 percent of what they live on. Absent that monthly check, nearly half of current seniors would fall below the poverty line.

Virtually no one quarrels with either those achievements, or the values they reflect. Instead, the debate is over how best to sustain them because the aging of America is seriously straining the system's finances. The ratio of current workers to retirees has been falling for decades, from 16:1 in 1950 to 3:1 in 2016, and is projected to be 2:1 by 2035 (Figure 2.1). At the same time, life expectancies for retirees are rising. From 1960 to 2020, life expectancy for Americans who reach age 65 will grow by six years—from 14.3 to 20.3 years. That's an increase of roughly 42 percent in the time these retirees will collect Social Security. Demographic forces like these move slowly, like a glacier, but with inexorable force.

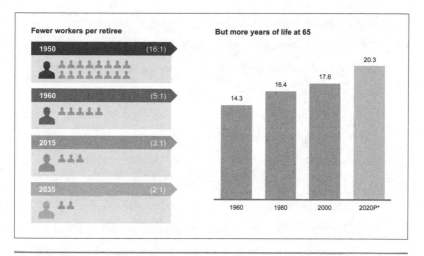

FIGURE 2.1 The demographic squeeze on Social Security

Source: 2016 Social Security Trustees Report; Center for Disease Control and Prevention (data based on death certificates), 2020 Projection from National Center for Health Statistics, "An Unhealthy America: Economic Burden of Chronic Disease" (2007), Milken Institute.

Indeed, Social Security is far along down a very predictable, and avoidable, path to crisis. If Congress doesn't act, the system will face a drop-off in benefits of over 20 percent by 2034 or sooner. We've known as far back as the 1990s that this cliff-drop in benefits was coming. But the political leadership needed to bring the system into sustainable balance has long been absent, despite a widespread consensus on what needs to be done.

The Most Predictable Crisis

Fully a generation ago, in their 1996 annual report, the Social Security system's Trustees warned, "The OASDI program is not in close actuarial balance. . . . The combined OASI and DI Trust funds would become exhausted in 2029 without corrective legislation. . . . At that time, annual tax revenue . . . would be sufficient to cover only 77 percent of annual expenditures." Not surprisingly, that warning went unheeded, largely because a shortfall then 33 years in the future had no political urgency.

Three presidents and 10 Congresses later, with no action having been taken to shore the system up, the 2016 Trustees report rang the warning bell again: "The combined trust funds will be depleted in 2034. . . . Thereafter, scheduled tax income is projected to be sufficient to pay about three-quarters of scheduled benefits." This time, though, the cliff-drop in retirement benefits was forecast just 18 years in the future. And the clock keeps ticking.

As multiple bipartisan commissions have shown in recent years, the compromises needed to restore Social Security to fiscal health are blindingly obvious, namely a balanced combination of revenue increases and benefit cuts. Among serious policy experts, the intellectual challenge of saving Social Security is widely seen as simple, back-of-the-envelope arithmetic—a policy layup far simpler than healthcare policy's three-level chess game of moral, financial, and scientific variables. But then politics has to be factored into the equation.

And serious action to ensure Social Security's long-term solvency has always been politically risky. An old, but all too true, sense of conventional Washington, D.C., wisdom holds that Social Security is too politically risky to reform. That's one reason we blew a golden opportunity to save Social Security during Bill Clinton's presidency in a lost retirement reform in 1998 (see box, "The Lost Retirement Reform of 1998").

Again, just over a decade ago, President George W. Bush's attempt to introduce private investment accounts as part of an overall Social Security reform failed utterly, and that failure stalled his entire second term's momentum. President Obama seemed to have drawn a lesson; over two full terms in office, he made no serious attempt to reform Social Security at all.

The Lost Retirement Reform of 1998

Reforms in programs as politically sensitive as Social Security require more than just pressing needs, accurate analyses, and wise policy solutions. They need political forces to come into an alignment of interests, if not trust, that makes compromise on politically lethal issues possible. But one reason to believe that comprehensive retirement reform in America is possible is that it very nearly happened—a generation ago.

Oklahoma University historian Steven Gillon tells the story of that missed opportunity in his book *The Pact*, which examines the rivalry and collaboration between President Bill Clinton and then-House Speaker Newt Gingrich. For a fleeting moment in 1998, right after fighting their way to a balanced budget agreement that produced the first federal budget surpluses in decades, these two brilliant policy wonks came within an inch of crafting a deal that would have been a huge step forward in American retirement policy.

Over the course of multiple secret meetings, the two men and their top staffs hammered out a compromise solution for retirement savings that would have made

Social Security solvent for the next 75 years, while also creating a universal, mandatory system of individual savings accounts for all workers as a private add-on to the public system. Driven by the desire to achieve an historic legacy achievement, both men were prepared to defy their parties' bases to lead a centrist coalition that would have begun by reforming retirement policy, and then moved on to reform Medicare and Medicaid.

President Clinton was prepared to defy the Democratic Party's orthodoxy in two ways: first, by including some substantial reductions in the scheduled growth of future Social Security benefits; second, by endorsing individual investment accounts to supplement the public program. For his part, Gingrich was prepared to defy the widespread Republican dogma of no new taxes by supporting significant new tax revenues to shore up Social Security's finances.

Professor Gillon writes that, even with coordinated support from two of the most powerful political figures in America, "a massive overhaul of Social Security would have been an uphill fight." Yet as the year 1998 opened, it was a genuine possibility. Hands had been shaken, words of honor given.

Then, on January 21, 1998, less than a week before Clinton's scheduled State of the Union rollout, news broke of the president's extramarital affair with a young White House intern, Monica Lewinsky. The deal was almost instantly dead on the GOP side, as the Lewinsky story dragged on through 1998 and turned from sex and lies to charges of perjury and eventually to impeachment. Clinton became totally dependent on a core political base of liberal Democrats in Congress, the group most suspicious of any reform that would include individual investment accounts. Any deal was off.

With Social Security long described as the "third rail" of American politics—"Touch it and you die!"—it had once again proved untouchable. But anyone looking back on this historic lost opportunity has to regret that this brief window for reform slammed shut so grotesquely.

Complicating the Search for Compromise

One reason that politicians hesitate to take on Social Security reform is that the system's basic structure is confusing even to experts, and impossible to distill to a sound bite or bumper sticker. The formulas used to define benefits are arcane. There are bookkeeping gimmicks like the Social Security Trust Funds; these funds consist of special-purpose government bonds issued by the Treasury exclusively to the Social Security Administration (SSA) to cover tax moneys that Treasury "borrowed" from the "surplus" revenues that SSA collected from the 1980s until 2014. That's when actual cash-flow surpluses ended, and SSA began to spend more in benefits than it took in as tax revenue. Talk about confusing!

None of this is easy to explain to a skeptical public. Voters rarely reward politicians who tell them they need to make sacrifices. Complicating the search for compromise, Social Security is ground zero for bitter clashes of ideologies and values: community versus individualism, solidarity versus economic freedom, Democrat versus Republican. Bridging those deep emotional divides won't be easy. But a secure retirement for generations to come will depend on politicians making compromises, and voters supporting them for doing so.

As a businessman who has devoted a career to building up private workplace savings in America, I've pored over decades of data on working Americans' savings patterns, their net worth, and their ability to replace their working incomes for life. And what I've seen convinces me that Social Security provides a uniquely valuable, irreplaceable base for everything else we do to encourage private retirement savings.

Precisely because Social Security relies exclusively on taxes drawn from labor income, we must supplement it with a system of investment accounts that can capture capital income as well—interest, dividends, and capital gains. The good news is that America's public and private retirement finance systems actually complement and reinforce each other in ways that few nations have achieved. (See box, "America's Twin-Engine Retirement Finance System," later in this chapter.)

Pay-as-You-Go: A Fateful Decision

To understand why we need to restore Social Security's solvency and also supplement the system with near-universal access to private workplace savings, it helps to look back at the system's origins in the depths of the Great Depression.

When the Social Security Act of 1935 was adopted, the United States became the last major industrial nation to join a wave of social insurance reform that began in Europe in the 1870s and only reached the United States amid the catastrophic unemployment and social unrest of the Depression.

That dire economic situation forced the policy architects of Social Security to make a fateful choice. To mitigate truly wrenching poverty among elderly Americans, they needed to get incoming revenue back out quickly. So the system's founders were forced to adopt a pay-as-you-go structure for the program. This meant that as payroll taxes were collected, they went directly from the Treasury to the Trust Funds run by the Social Security Administration (SSA), which were then used to pay current beneficiaries.

In the debates leading up to the 1935 act, Congress had seriously weighed the idea of creating a prefunded retirement system. Such a system, like most pension plans, would have invested in stocks and bonds, accumulated investment earnings, and used those earnings to pay future benefits. But the need to get money out fast, compounded by the fear and loathing of Wall Street that followed the Great Crash of 1929, made the option of investing in the real economy and then waiting years for returns to build up significantly before paying benefits deeply unappealing. Many early beneficiaries, after all, were aging and destitute veterans of the First World War.

This decision to pay out immediately was good news, even great news, for the system's first beneficiaries. They got immediate relief without having paid much in taxes. Miss Ida May Fuller, who received the very first Social Security check in 1940—for $22.54—had only paid $24.75 into the infant system during her whole working life. She lived to be 100 years old and collected more than $20,000 from Social Security during her lifetime.

But the fabulous rate of return that Miss Fuller and her cohort received from Social Security has been declining steadily ever since. That's because as a pay-as-you-go system matures, more people spend their whole working lives paying in. And since their taxes are not invested, but instead are used to pay current beneficiaries, their own future benefits can't take advantage of long-term compounding of interest or stock market growth. Instead, they depend on tax flows from *future* generations of workers and on changes to taxes and benefits enacted by Congress and signed by presidents.

Congress and various administrations have, in fact, frequently tweaked Social Security's taxes and benefit levels over the years. From the Eisenhower era in the 1950s through the Nixon years in the 1970s, the trend was to expand the number of people covered by the system, raise their benefits, or both. Richard Nixon's administration, for example, indexed future benefits to gains in workers' wages, which typically rise slightly faster than the CPI.

By the early 1970s, though, the benefit creep that made Social Security such a great deal for those born before World War II was winding down. By contrast, reforms enacted in 1977 and 1983, when the system twice veered toward financial crisis, have all trimmed back on benefits rather than expanding them by changing payout formulas for lifetime earnings or raising the retirement age for full benefits to 67.

The last major reform of Social Security, in 1983, based on recommendations from a commission headed by future Federal

Reserve chief Alan Greenspan, included one of the largest long-term tax increases in American history. That set the Federal Insurance Contributions Act (FICA) taxes that fund Social Security on track to rise from 10.8 percent of payroll in 1983 to the current level of 12.4 percent, while full retirement age was set to rise gradually from 65 to 67, a substantial reduction in benefits.

In theory, half of these taxes come from employers, half from employees. In economic reality, though, all the taxes are experienced by employers as part of the overall cost of hiring labor. So they actually reduce workers' potential take-home pay dollar for dollar. And Social Security taxes have consistently ratcheted up, never down. Today, more than three-quarters of American families pay more in payroll taxes than in income taxes.

By law, Social Security has no private investments comparable to the stocks and bonds held by private pension plans. Instead, and by design, its benefits have traditionally been paid mostly by FICA taxes on wages, supplemented by any interest that SSA earns on the special, nonmarketable, interest-bearing Treasury obligations it holds in its Trust Funds.

Franklin Roosevelt and the New Deal architects of Social Security firmly believed that keeping the system "off budget," having it be financed almost exclusively by the tax contributions that workers themselves paid in, would strengthen its political legitimacy and make it nearly impossible for future Congresses to cut back. To a large extent, FDR's vision has proved correct. The problem is that this sense of entitlement has also made Social Security very difficult to reform, even as its long-term ability to self-fund is steadily eroding.

Social Security for the Well-to-Do

Everyone knows that Social Security is vital to low-to-moderate and middle-income families. And we can safely assume that for the richest of the rich—decamillionaires on up—the income they receive from the system will represent just a minuscule fraction of their lifestyle costs. What we may not realize is just how far up the wealth ladder we can go and still find significant value from that monthly check, even for affluent families.

Consider a hypothetical couple, now age 67. After long and successful careers, they have no debts or mortgage payments. Their children's college loans are paid off. And their $2 million in retirement savings places them well into the top one-tenth of all Americans their age for net worth. In fact, they have more money than 95 percent of their peers.

You might think that Social Security doesn't matter much to them. You would be dead wrong. Because, as their financial advisor tells them, the traditional "4 percent rule" for safe asset drawdowns means they should take only $80,000 a year from their $2 million in savings without incurring too much risk. The good news, the advisor adds, is that after decades of paying top-level Social Security taxes, they also qualify for $3,400 a month in Social Security benefits, or over $40,000 a year including a built-in cost-of-living adjustment for life. In short, this well-heeled couple will depend on Social Security for a third or more of their lifetime income.

The advisor offers one note of caution. Unless Congress acts to make the system solvent, their annual

> Social Security earning could drop overnight by well over
> $10,000 a year in 2034, just as they are reaching age
> 85. But not to worry: "Surely Congress and the president
> would never, ever, let that happen." Would they?

Today, roughly 10,000 baby boomers reach age 65 every day; meanwhile, the number of active workers per retiree has been declining for decades. But Social Security's pay-as-you-go structure still reflects mortality and family patterns of the 1930s, an era of large families, rising populations, and short life spans. When the Social Security retirement age was set at 65 in the 1930s, for example, life expectancy was just over 61 for American men and 65 for women.

As of 2015, these mounting pressures brought Social Security into cash-flow deficit, with the system now paying out more in benefits than it takes in from FICA taxes; the shortfall is made up by drawing on the special bonds in its Trust Funds. These are unique, nontradable, intragovernmental debts. What are assets to Social Security are liabilities for the Treasury. So when SSA puts these bonds to Treasury for payment, Treasury has to pay these debts, just as it pays off any other bond, from general tax revenue or from the proceeds of new borrowing.

But unless current law is changed, even today's more than $2.8 trillion in Trust Fund assets will diminish steadily to zero sometime in the early 2030s. From the moment Social Security went into negative cash flow and began drawing on its Trust Fund holdings, the system's FICA tax income began covering a smaller and smaller portion of its obligations to retirees each year. That FICA share will drop from roughly 99 percent in

2014 to about 75 percent by 2034, when the system's trustees project that the Trust Funds will be exhausted. At that point, the system would be technically insolvent—that is, unable to pay its promised benefits in full. Current law would then require an across-the-board drop in benefits variously estimated at between 21 percent and 25 percent.

That doesn't mean that Social Security will ever go bankrupt. By definition, a pay-as-you-go system can't go bankrupt. Even assuming *no* reform to current law, the Social Security Administration has a claim on 12.4 percent of future U.S. payroll, a very tidy sum indeed, which would enable it to deliver between three-quarters and four-fifths of promised benefits. But once the Trust Funds are depleted, a sudden 20 percent to 25 percent cut in benefits would deliver a devastating blow to tens of millions of retirees, survivors, orphans, and the disabled, plunging many into near-destitution and squandering decades of progress in reducing elderly poverty.

What Needs to Be Done

To prevent such a human policy disaster, our political leaders can choose among an array of options for increasing tax revenues to SSA, reducing future benefit increases programmed in current law, or securing higher rates of return for assets in the Social Security Trust Funds.

In 2011, I collaborated on just such a solution in partnership with James Roosevelt, then CEO of Tufts Health Plan, a former associate commissioner of the Social Security system and Franklin Roosevelt's grandson. Our policy proposals, published in an op-ed in the *Boston Globe* (see Appendix B: "How to Fix Social Security") were an almost exact balance between adding revenues and reducing the growth of future benefits.

You, Too, Can Save Social Security!

If you would like to try saving Social Security yourself, you can find an excellent, easy-to-use online planning tool called The Reformer: An Interactive Tool to Fix Social Security (http://crfb.org/socialsecurityreformer/). It allows you to model changes in taxes, benefit formulas, and other policy options, most of them involving some degree of sacrifice. But The Reformer also offers the option of directing a share of the system's Trust Fund assets into stock investments, a fairly painless choice that could close about one-fifth of the system's long-term funding gap all by itself.

Whatever mix of policies you might support, it's critical to recognize that saving Social Security is overwhelmingly a *political* problem, since both its revenues and its benefits are set by Congress. To say that the system faces a long-term funding shortfall, or is headed for insolvency, simply means that Congress has failed to bring its revenue into line with its promises. Fixing Social Security is a job for Congress and will likely require strong presidential leadership to get moving.

To have any chance of passage, any fix will almost surely require a balanced combination of added revenues and reductions in future benefit increases. Democrats won't accept a reform made up exclusively of benefit cuts; Republicans won't

accept one made up wholly of tax increases. Anyone proposing such one-sided reforms is actually aiming for stalemate,
no action, and ultimately, insolvency. Having no viable reform
plan is, in fact, itself a plan for failure.

The most politically viable way to secure a bipartisan reform
would be to follow the path last traveled in 1983—a presidential commission with representatives from both parties, and
independent experts who are charged with producing reforms
that Congress can vote up or down, but not amend.

Recent years have seen a number of such balanced reform
plans advanced. The Simpson-Bowles Commission brought
one forward in 2010. So did a study led by former Senator Pete
Domenici and former Budget Director Alice Rivlin. Again, in
2016, the Bipartisan Policy Center delivered a comprehensive
retirement savings plan that covered both Social Security and
private workplace systems.

Each of these plans found that it would be possible to make
Social Security solvent for the indefinite future mainly by slowing the rate of growth of future benefits for those above median
income and by raising the cap on income taxed under FICA to
cover roughly 90 percent of wages. What's more, it would also
be possible to step up the baseline minimum payment to above-
poverty income levels and add some additional benefits for the
very old—people over, say, 85.

In short, these reforms would actually make Social Security
somewhat more progressive and more effective at prevent-
ing poverty in late old age. Any one of these reform packages
would, of course, be vastly better for most people than having
the system drift steadily toward a 20-percent-plus drop in benefits by the 2030s. And time is not on our side. Delay causes

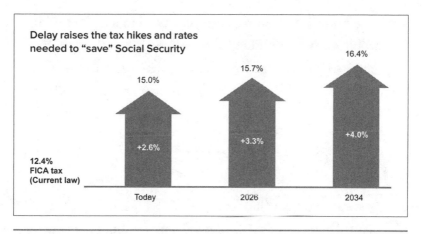

Delay raises the tax hikes and rates needed to "save" Social Security

16.4%

15.7%

15.0%

+4.0%

+3.3%

+2.6%

12.4%
FICA tax
(Current law)

Today   2026   2034

FIGURE 2.2   Time is not on our side

Source: Social Security Administration, Committee for a Responsible Federal Budget calculations.

the system's funding gap to grow steadily wider, and then will require deeper and more painful tax hikes or benefit cuts in the future, as Figure 2.2 illustrates.

However necessary, relatively painless, and even beneficial any proposed Social Security reform may be, getting it started will take real courage on the part of political leaders. As with every other issue in our fractured republic, changes to Social Security will be hotly contested and feature a tsunami of lies, fearmongering, and exaggeration. It's not easy to take even the first step toward reform for politicians who may find themselves pilloried—and "primaried"—just for contemplating benefit cuts or tax increases.

We can only hope that a new constellation of strong leadership and real political courage will emerge that is willing to take up America's retirement finance challenge again. And we can urge members of Congress to step up. If and when they do, these brave men and women are going to need help, from every one of us, to get the job done. As citizens, voters, party members, donors, businesspeople, or workers, all of us should urge our elected officials to take on the challenge of Social Security solvency, make real compromises, and cut a fair deal. The sooner they act, the better.

Longevity and Social Security: The Ultimate Inequality

Policy analysts seeking to shore up Social Security's finances often suggest raising the national retirement age. However, while this benefit cut would significantly lower the system's costs, most of the sacrifice would come from the pockets of lower-income workers who depend most on Social Security. Here's why.

Increasing life expectancy is surely a near-unalloyed positive, even if it does put stress on our retirement savings systems and Social Security. But the system's advocates have long celebrated the way it redistributes wealth by replacing a higher share of preretirement incomes for lower-paid workers than it does for higher earners. At the point of retirement, this still holds true.

Over time, though, as workers draw from the system, this redistributive effect steadily erodes. That's because Social Security, like any annuitized system, also redistributes benefits from those who die early to those who live longer. If two workers have identical benefits, the one who collects for 20 years receives more than twice as much as the worker who dies after 10 years.

This second form of redistribution was little noted because until the 1970s, both lower- and higher-income workers had similar life expectancies at retirement. Death was an equal opportunity risk across income classes. That is no longer the case. As American income and wealth inequality has deepened over recent decades, life expectancy has also begun to diverge—sharply—across the income spectrum. This might be thought of as the ultimate inequality.

Today, at age 65, workers in the top half of the income spectrum, men and women alike, stand to live more than five years longer than their peers in the bottom half. At the polar extremes of income, the U.S. Health Inequality Project found this gap to be even wider. The highest-paid 5 percent of workers today stand to live *12 years* longer than the lowest-paid 5 percent (Figure 2.3).

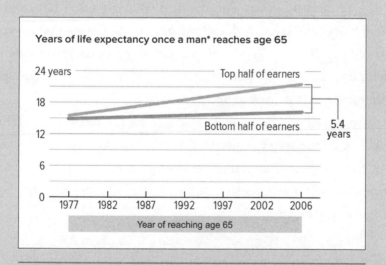

Years of life expectancy once a man* reaches age 65

FIGURE 2.3 Life expectancy rising faster for higher earners

*Male workers covered by Social Security.

Sources: Hilary Waldron, "Trends in Mortality Differentials and Life Expectancy for Male Social Security-Covered Workers, by Socioeconomic Status," *Social Security Bulletin*, Nov. 2007; Center on Budget and Policy Priorities, 2016. http://www.cbpp.org

The implications for Social Security are clear. Higher life expectancy for well-to-do workers is fast eroding the progressivity of the system simply because better-paid retirees collect benefits for years longer. In this context, one often-noted idea, raising the early or full benefit retirement age for Social Security access, would just exacerbate an already growing inequality in retirement finance and end up hurting lower-income workers the most.

As we develop retirement policy, we need to take this trend into account so as not to make a difficult situation worse. We are already seeing signs of real financial stress among elders who are far into retirement and whose assets have drained down. MIT economist James Poterba and colleagues at Dartmouth and Harvard's John F. Kennedy School of Government estimated in a 2012 study that 46 percent of senior citizens now die with less than $10,000 to their names. Most of them depended almost entirely on Social Security to live.

So if policy makers do choose to raise the retirement age to help make the system solvent, a strong case can be made to offset the "ultimate inequality" of diverging longevity with some form of new, means-tested supplemental income benefits for those living beyond, say, age 80.

America's Twin-Engine Retirement Finance System

Retirement income in America is drawn from two very different and complementary sources: human capital and financial capital. Our key public retirement system, Social Security, is fueled by taxes on labor income (wages and salaries). Private retirement savings, mainly through workplace savings plans like 401(k)s or IRAs, draw on investment returns from capital markets. That means these plans capture the interest, dividends, and capital gains due to owners of stocks, bonds, and other investment securities.

No one consciously planned it, but by blending these diverse and variable income sources, the United States has created a robust hybrid structure, a reasonably well-balanced twin-engine vehicle for financing retirement. Given the right reforms, this hybrid system can offer American workers and retirees more substantial, sustainable, and flexible retirement incomes than any purely private or purely public system likely could.

To see what diversification of income sources means, let's compare the growth of the wage base from which Social Security draws tax revenues to the rise of the Standard & Poor's 500 stock index—a fair proxy for the stock market returns that most workplace savings plans offer as a core investment option (Figure 2.4).

We can clearly see that the wage base that Social Security relies on for tax revenues has been rising slowly but steadily for decades. Over the two generations since 1970, it is up by about 130 percent in real terms, with only minimal downturns during recessions. By contrast, the S&P 500 has risen vastly more since 1970, by over 1,000 percent. But America's stock markets have seen some unnerving roller-coaster swings

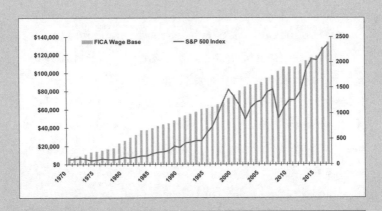

FIGURE 2.4 Retirement income sources: diversification between FICA wages and stock market returns

Sources: S&P 500 Index and FICA wage base.

along the way, including two severe market crashes in this young millennium.

What we haven't seen, despite these sharp drops, is any mass panic by 401(k) savers. Some did, of course, cash out at market bottoms. But most workers continued to invest in the markets paycheck by paycheck. These savers effectively rode out the crashes, adding more equity to their holdings at a discount while waiting for markets to rebound.

One reason so many workplace savers in America have, in fact, managed to endure and recover from recent market drops is simply this: they know that whatever markets do, they can also count on an inflation-protected annuity from Social Security for the rest of their lives. That knowledge significantly mitigates over-all risk.

In short, and again, with no planning, the United States has created a well-diversified portfolio of retirement income sources. We link flows from a steady, low-volatility source like wages to returns from faster-rising but far more volatile securities markets. This is consistent with Modern Portfolio Theory (MPT), which tells us that diversification of risk (not putting all your eggs in one basket) is key to sustaining returns from an investment portfolio.

U.S. defined contribution (DC) retirement savings now constitute a multitrillion-dollar national savings portfolio, formed by tens of millions of individual workers' accounts, an unplanned masterpiece of diversification. This vast accumulation of DC retirement savings relieves pressure on our Social Security system, which itself enables workers to take greater risks and earn higher returns on their private savings.

America's twin-engine retirement finance system is unique in the world. It is arguably more stable than retirement systems that rely solely on tax revenues or on private investments alone. Retirement systems built solely on wage-funded social insurance are unable to take advantage of the powerful dynamics of capital market growth. Systems that are almost wholly made up by private mandatory savings (such as Australia's) offer minimal social insurance backup. But America's public/private hybrid retirement system manages to link social insurance flows with market returns in a way that's diversified, sustainable, and stable.

That said, we do have major work to do in tuning up both engines. The good news is that what needs to be done is crystal clear. We know that only a balanced mix of increased revenue and modified benefits has any chance politically to bring Social Security into long-term fiscal solvency. And we know that to finish the job on the private side, we must extend access for all Americans workers to well-designed, automatic payroll savings plans with savings rates high enough to enable them to replace their work-life incomes when they retire. Implementing these changes is a political challenge, not an economic or intellectual one. We have the resources; all we need is the will.

CHAPTER 3

HOW DID WE GET HERE? THE RISE OF DEFINED CONTRIBUTION SAVINGS

From tiny seeds a mighty tree may grow.
—AESCHYLUS

To understand how we evolved the workplace savings systems that Americans rely on today, we need to look back more than 40 years. It also helps to recall how "the law of unintended consequences" plays out.

All legislation and regulations have consequences. The intended ones are typically immediate and foreseen; the unintended ones are often totally unforeseen, but may have powerful, even revolutionary, long-term effects. This is very much the case with two 1970s laws that helped set off an unplanned, almost accidental transformation in American retirement finance.

The first was **The Employee Retirement Income Security Act of 1974** (ERISA), which was adopted to address a wave of private pension failures, notably the 1963 bankruptcy of the Studebaker Corporation that cost thousands of workers and retirees their pension incomes. ERISA aimed to set high standards and practices for traditional defined benefit pension plans. It also created the federal government's Pension Benefit Guaranty Corporation (PBGC) to insure and backstop pension payments. But its long-term unintended effect, as we'll see, was to start a lasting decline in traditional pensions.

The second law that seeded change was the **Revenue Act of 1978**, a seemingly routine adjustment of tax brackets and rates. But this 1978 law included an obscure provision, barely noticed at the time, but now world-famous: **section 401(k) of the Internal Revenue Code**. This allowed employees to defer taxes on a portion of income provided they set that money aside for their retirement. Ultimately, this 401(k) tweak in the tax code gave birth to a whole new defined contribution industry. In short, two laws designed to protect and extend the defined benefit pension status quo actually launched a revolution.

Intended to bolster traditional pensions, ERISA inadvertently sped up a transition away from them. It created new and sometimes expensive mandates for plan sponsors, raising minimum standards for participation, vesting, and funding. By establishing the Pension Benefit Guaranty Corporation, it added some reliability to traditional plans, but at a cost of higher and rising insurance payments and compliance costs. The unintended effect was to encourage many plan sponsors to seek other ways to offer retirement coverage to their workers. And a viable alternative came quite soon, embedded in the Revenue Act of 1978.

By providing a personally owned, tax-advantaged alternative to traditional pensions, section 401(k) planted the seed for the multitrillion-dollar defined contribution savings that have grown up over the past two generations and reshaped retirement finance in the United States and, increasingly, around the world.

The availability of personal payroll-deduction retirement savings options did not spur an immediate gold rush into these new 401(k) accounts. At first, just a handful of large companies began offering K-plans as supplements to their traditional pensions, offering them at first mostly to senior executives. Looking back, it's comical to recall the clunky, off-putting name that most early sponsors gave to these savings options: "salary reduction plans." Not much marketing genius in that name!

Yet by the early 1980s, thousands of employers across America had begun to realize the potential of 401(k) plans and individual workers' accounts to become a mass-investing retirement savings vehicle for almost all workers, not just executives. Better still, and unlike traditional pensions, the costs of these plans would be entirely predictable.

That's because K-plans, by definition, shift investment risk from the plan sponsor to the individual participant. They promise no more than the potential income that can be drawn from participants' accumulated balances. This means that they are, again by definition, fully funded by the contributions of employees along with any matching funds an employer may choose to offer.

The benefits of such plans to employers seem crystal clear: total predictability and limited liability. But 401(k)s and defined contribution plans like 403(b)s and 457s also proved immensely appealing to millions of workers who saw their personal wealth begin to grow in their regular plan statements.

The 18-year boom in equity markets that ran, with a few sharp breaks, from 1982 to 2000 provided a powerful tailwind to the rapid growth of a defined contribution industry that included plan sponsors, record keepers, investment managers, consultants, and advisors.

And this surge was further stimulated by legislation that established nondiscrimination rules that required plan sponsors to share the benefits of workplace savings plans with nearly all employees, not just the highly compensated.

The Rise of Workplace Savings 1.0

From the mid-1980s straight through to the century's end, a steadily increasing share of America's leading companies moved to convert their retirement benefit offerings from traditional pensions to defined contribution savings plans.

What started as a trickle soon swelled to a flood. This first generation of payroll deduction plans—what we'll call Workplace Savings 1.0—was well underway, and it grew explosively. Thousands of companies adopted the new plans, and a growing array of service providers started to compete for their business by offering an ever-growing range of investment choices, options, and customer services.

The transition from traditional pensions to defined contribution plans was driven by market pressures to control costs, and by demand from employees themselves. Increasingly mobile workers liked the fact that these new plans offered rapid or immediate vesting. Others appreciated the strong sense of personal ownership these plans provided. As of 1990, more

American workers were enrolled in DC plans than in traditional final-pay pensions.

By the mid-decade of the 1990s more than 40 million workers owned over $1.3 trillion in workplace retirement savings accounts and IRAs. Most new cash flowing into IRAs came in the form of substantial rollovers into these accounts from workplace savings plans, at retirement or at the time of job changes, not from individual contributions that people actively chose to deposit in small increments.

Regulatory oversight of the emerging defined contribution plan system took another big step with the passage of the Economic Growth and Tax Reconciliation Act of 2001 (EGTRA), which allowed for additional catch-up savings for employees over 50 years old and created Roth 401(k)s, which enabled employees to make after-tax contributions that are taxed upon withdrawal the way ordinary 401(k) funds are. This offered another strategic option for savers and financial planners to consider.

More recently, the **Pension Protection Act of 2006 (PPA)** capped 20 years of retirement policy evolution by endorsing a series of best practices in workplace savings plans that had been inspired by behavioral finance research and experiments by a handful of progressive plan sponsors. The PPA, in effect, marked the first time that Congress and top policy makers recognized defined contribution plans as the primary source of future retirement income and acted to treat these plans as a system. (We'll learn more about why PPA marks such a remarkable leap forward in retirement policy in the next chapter.)

Today, traditional pension plans and defined contribution savings continue to coexist. Some large companies continue to

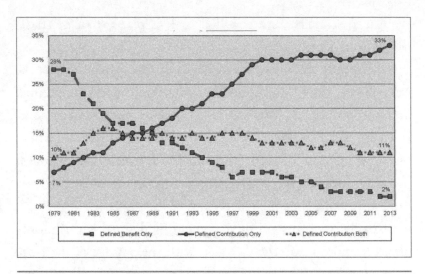

FIGURE 3.1   Private sector workers participating in an employment-based retirement plan, by plan type, 1979-2013, among all workers

Source: U.S. Department of Labor Form 5500 Summaries 1979–1998, Pension Guaranty Corporation, EBRI.

fund and sustain defined benefit plans, but they are a shrinking minority. By contrast, the flood of assets fueling America's defined contribution savings engine shows no sign of abating. Both types of plan continue to evolve, but in very different ways, as we'll see.

Traditional Defined Benefit Pensions

Some analysts, and especially critics of America's retirement system, claim that until quite recently, this country enjoyed a "Golden Age" of defined benefit pensions. To hear them tell it, most American workers enjoyed turnkey financial security for life; then, the self-seeking leadership of corporate America threw these workers to the wolves of the financial services world, leaving them to fend for themselves and manage their own retirement through risky, high-cost 401(k) plans. This is nonsense on steroids, the academic and journalistic equivalent of an urban legend.

Let me say that I have nothing against defined benefit pension plans, provided they are well run, have fair rules, and are fully funded. All through my career, I have worked for companies that serve such plans. Many traditional pensions are rock solid and offer great benefits to long-serving workers.

But the notion that DB plans were ever near-universal is a myth. And nostalgia for that myth distracts us from acting to improve the DC plans that have replaced them. Here are the facts.

At their high-water mark in the early 1990s, traditional pensions, which deliver retirement benefits based on salary and years of service, only covered 35 percent of private sector American workers, mostly at large, national scale Fortune 500 firms. Most companies that offered these DB plans required years, sometimes as long as a decade or more, to vest the ownership of retirement assets and future income for any individual worker. Income benefits in retirement were usually calculated in a way that provided huge gains based on the last decade or so of a worker's career, typically from age 50 to 65. Younger workers' vested income rights grew slowly for many years and would most often be cashed out, or even forfeited, if they left before full retirement age.

Tens of millions of workers who changed jobs prior to vesting never received a penny's worth of benefits. Contributions made on their behalf to the DB pension pool wound up sweetening the pensions of long-serving "lifers." What's more, most of these traditional pensions were tied to a single employer. They weren't portable; you couldn't take them with you when you changed jobs.

Those who cling to the notion that our retirees were better off in the age of defined benefit need to face up to actual real-world data. Virtually all the key indicators of elders' welfare today are superior to those seen a generation ago. Well along into the defined contribution era, we have less elderly poverty, better elderly health, longer life expectancy, and even superior measures of happiness among elders than we had a generation ago when defined benefit pensions were at their peak.

Over recent decades, the U.S. economy has grown increasingly dynamic. We routinely see companies and even entire economic sectors expanding, contracting, and even disappearing. Fast-growing upstarts regularly eclipse markets and roll out new technologies. Workers themselves hold 8 to 10 jobs over a typical career. In this new reality, the limitations of DB plans with their multidecade vesting provisions are striking.

That's why virtually all of the fastest-growing companies that have emerged over the past generation—in information technology, mobile broadband, finance, life sciences, digital networks, renewable energy, and the like—haven't chosen to offer defined benefit pensions. Facebook, Apple, Microsoft, Amazon, Netflix, and Google have only ever offered defined contribution plans.

Most remaining DB plans today are concentrated in a dwindling number of long-established incumbent firms in mature industries with a high proportion of union membership (oil, autos, airlines) and in the public sector (also, in many states, a union mainstay). Even in these areas, the future of defined benefit plans is not promising.

While there is great disparity among DB plans in terms of their relative levels of funding and viability, taken as a whole, U.S. defined benefit pension plans are saddled with unfunded liabilities that measure in the trillions of dollars. That simply means that companies or government agencies in too many cases have not set aside enough money to reliably pay the benefits to retirees that these plans promise on paper.

Private sector DB plans face chronic underfunding of some $300 billion. In fact, the Pension Benefit Guaranty Corporation established by ERISA to insure and backstop such plans may itself soon face insolvency unless Congress acts to provide it with more funding.

In the public sector, while many DB plans are healthy and on track to match liabilities, many others—notably the massive state plans in New Jersey, Illinois, and California—will almost certainly be unable to deliver benefits that those states' political leaders (many now retired) promised these government workers. Several states' pension systems are underfunded by 50 percent or more. In aggregate, public sector DB plans face unfunded liabilities of nearly $5 trillion, and highly predictable crises loom in the near future.

Public DB plans are being weighed down by a classic "support ratio" challenge. Rising numbers of retirees depend on contributions from fewer active workers. Underfunded pension pools face liabilities owed to growing numbers of retirees, often against a backdrop of flat or declining tax bases. An aging demographic is the primary culprit, driving serious and intractable municipal and state debts and deficits.

Even current monetary policy threatens DB plans' prospects. The zero-interest-rate environment that has prevailed in the wake of the global financial crisis is severely stressing traditional pension plans' liability models. Historically low interest rates create a powerful drag on public pension plans that invest heavily in fixed-income instruments. The lower the interest rate, the lower the returns and therefore the greater the difficulty in matching liabilities.

These trends combine to create a perfect storm with potentially tragic consequences for millions of private and public sector workers whose defined benefit retirement income may not be forthcoming. For governments and corporations, the costs of continuing to provide secure defined benefit pensions can threaten their ability to invest in innovation and crowd out essential services. The choice can even boil down to current staffing or current pensions, a choice between keeping police and firefighters on the job today versus paying full benefits to those who served their communities in the past.

Defined benefit pensions may have been suited to a slower changing, less volatile economy in which workers were accustomed to job tenure measured in decades. Today, they often seem like an artifact from another time. By contrast, defined contribution savings are robust and surging.

The Defined Contribution Tsunami

From the perspective of a career largely dedicated since the mid-1980s to spurring the growth of defined contribution retirement savings, my timing was extremely lucky. I caught a wave.

In 1985, defined contribution savings plans accounted for only $427 billion—less than half the assets to be found in defined benefit pension plans. Over the next 10 years, DC assets under management soared by about 12 percent a year, quadrupling to $1.3 trillion by 1995, while traditional pension assets grew about 5 percent, still healthy, but losing overall market share.

The explosion of DC assets continued unabated, despite the dot.com boom and bust at the turn of our century. As this transition gathered steam, it became obvious that a fundamental shift was taking place in American retirement finance. Individual workers, for the first time in history, were accruing substantial wealth of their own despite periodic bouts of market volatility that did little to set back the inexorable rise in individually held assets.

By 2005, DC and IRA assets were at parity with DB, at $7.4 trillion each. Only a dozen years later, in 2017, and again, despite the ravages of the 2008–2009 global financial crisis, defined contribution workplace savings plans and IRAs topped $15 trillion, over 75 percent more than the $8 trillion managed by traditional DB plans (Figure 3.2).

It *is* true that individual 401(k) savers' behavior can be more volatile than that of professional pension plan managers. Some individual investors have made serious mistakes in responding to market setbacks such as selling at the bottom during a stock market correction. But if we look at the behavior of defined contribution savers as a group, it's clear that workforce savers in aggregate manage periods of volatility nearly as well as those in traditional DB pension plans.

We've had several real-life stress tests in recent years, notably the historically unprecedented retreat of asset prices during

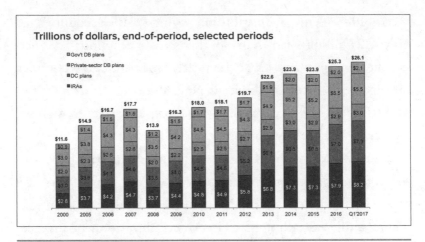

FIGURE 3.2 U.S. total retirement market assets

Source: ICI Total Retirement Assets, Fourth Quarter 2016.

the 2008–2009 global financial crisis. The market reversals of that period were unique, not only because of their severity, but because nearly every asset class—stocks, bonds, and even real estate—all retreated together in a massive "risk-off" trade, something that traditional risk models had not anticipated.

But even as that gut-wrenching volatility stressed markets worldwide, 401(k)-type plans actually held up better than traditional DB pensions. And as markets recovered from 2009 onward, defined contribution plan assets grew at nearly twice the rate of DB assets.

Between 2007 and 2008, when markets bore the full brunt of the crash, total DC plan assets fell by 12 percent, while DB plan valuations retreated by 14 percent. And over the first five years of recovery, from 2008 to 2013, traditional pension plan valuations increased by 41 percent, but DC workplace savings and IRA valuations soared by fully 78 percent due to both the market recovery and continuing flows of new contributions by workers and employers.

Calling a Draw on the
Pensions vs. 401(k) Debate

Capstone evidence that the transition from defined benefits pension to 401(k)-type savings plans has not eroded retirement security in America came in late 2015. Two of America's leading retirement research institutions effectively called a draw in the long-running debate over the outcomes of traditional pensions and the emerging DC savings system.

Boston College's Center for Retirement Research (CRR), in a 2015 report entitled "Investment Returns: Defined Benefit vs. Defined Contribution Plans," found that between 1990 and 2012, professionally managed DB plans outperformed DC plans by just 0.7 percent—with the differential accounted for mainly by higher fees on the DC side. But as we know, economies of scale and competitive market forces are steadily bringing down 401(k) fees, as total assets in these plans grow and competition to manage them becomes more intense.

While most traditional pensions are found in larger, often multibillion-dollar funds, the defined contribution market is mostly made up by tens of thousands of small and medium-sized workplace savings plans. The cost differential is real and challenging. But it is diminishing rapidly. New technologies, market competition, and the increasing use of index funds are all driving down the cost of defined contribution plans of all sizes. The BC Center's report also noted that more defined contribution savings tend to be allocated to equities, which means that they encounter both more risk and higher returns than the DB plans that lean more heavily on fixed-income investments.

The report marked a sharp course change for CRR, which, like many other academic analysts, had long believed that defined benefit plans provided markedly superior retirement readiness. As its authors concluded: "Our reading of the data . . . is that the accumulation of retirement assets has not declined as a result of the shift to defined contribution plans. We are going to have to change our story!"

Another 2015 report, from the Employee Benefit Research Institute (EBRI), went a major step further. EBRI assessed the likelihood that workers currently ages 25 to 29 would be able to replace at least 70 percent of their preretirement income through traditional final-pay defined benefit pensions or, alternatively, through 401(k) plans.

The findings were strikingly positive for those like me who have long been convinced that well-designed workplace savings plans can successfully deliver retirement readiness for most people. EBRI found, for example, that workers in the third and fourth income quartiles have a much higher probability of success with 401(k) plans than with DB plans. And if we raise the target replacement ratio to 80 percent, payroll savings plans have a much higher probability of success than DB plans for all workers except those in the lowest-income quartile, where results are a virtual tie. EBRI's report further found that workers in plans that applied automatic savings escalation would earn even higher rates of replacement.

EBRI's findings confirm my view that well-designed defined contribution plans can do at least as well, and very often much better, for workers' retirement readiness than traditional pensions. As I mentioned earlier: "There's nothing wrong with 401(k) plans that can't be fixed by what's right about 401(k)s."

America's Primary Retirement Savings Plan

Today, we are far along in the transition from traditional pensions, which served a minority well, to a system of individual payroll savings that can potentially enable almost all working Americas to reach retirement readiness. There's no going back. Defined benefit pensions will almost surely continue to flatline as their plan participants age and leave the workforce. Defined contribution plans will likely continue their expansion and, we hope, extend coverage to more workers and workplaces.

In a little over 30 years, we have already spread defined contribution retirement savings to a much larger share of American workers than traditional pensions ever touched. And by many measures, these plans are providing superior benefits—more sustainable, fully funded, and immune to many of the demographic pressures faced by traditional pension plans. These are amazing achievements.

But as 401(k)s and other payroll savings plans have become America's primary source of future retirement income, the deficits and flaws that affect far too many of these plans have become a major source of controversy and political vulnerability—some of it based on real failings.

Academics, theorists, and the financial media pore over the shortfalls and failings that pockmark the defined contribution landscape. But too few of these critics bother to note the successes and positive trends in the evolution of DC savings, even though these elements are equally visible and suggest proven pathways to improving the whole workplace saving system.

Here's what we know: Roughly half of American workers now enjoy access to 401(k)-type plans. Multiple polls tell us that these workers are very happy with their plans. Actuarial data tell us that millions of them are on track to be able to replace much, or even all, of their working life income once they retire.

A Job Half Done

Clearly, we face a challenge. Many of the defined benefit pensions still available today are sorely strained. Collectively, they face wrenching adjustments as funding shortfalls measured in the trillions of dollars stress many of these plans to the breaking point. Among private businesses, traditional pensions are disappearing fast. In the public sector, they present an enormous fiscal issue for many state and local governments. Indeed, some cities have actually declared bankruptcy largely as a result of unsustainable pension obligations.

In stark contrast, defined contribution savings plans do very well by middle- and upper-income workers. But they don't reach nearly as deeply as they could to serve low-income, part-time, or "contingent" workers or those in small firms that lack on-the-job payroll savings plans entirely.

The fact that roughly 35 percent of all American workers don't have such savings options is tragic. I would even say it's a scandal, a failure of imagination and empathy on the part of policy makers in this country. But that gap in coverage doesn't mean that the 401(k) workplace savings concept is broken or failing. What it means is that we need to extend coverage to all.

The job of fleshing out a workplace savings system for all Americans is only half done. But we are, to be fair, just about 30 years along in the great migration from defined benefit pensions to defined contribution models. Today's surviving DB plans reflect nineteenth-century designs. By contrast, the fast-evolving defined contribution system was pretty much invented from scratch—beginning in the 1980s—just as I was beginning my career.

To keep evolving, and improving, workplace savings in America, we surely do need to admit the flaws. But much more importantly—and constructively—we need to focus like a laser on the success stories and the structures, behaviors, and ideas that account for these successes. To lift America's workplace savings plans to a new level of efficiency and effectiveness, we should follow the advice that Alex Haley, the author of *Roots*, took as his motto: "Find the good and praise it."

As it happens, there is a shining example of wise thinking and bipartisan political compromise to guide us. Sadly, almost no one outside the retirement industry has ever heard of this legislative landmark. But 11 years after its adoption, this law is helping tens of millions of working families build a more solid financial foundation. Despite the dysfunction of Congress in recent years, the process that led to this law's passage offers us hope that our elected officials can sometimes work across party lines to improve all Americans' futures. So, in the next chapter, let's take a deeper look at this remarkable law, the Pension Protection Act of 2006.

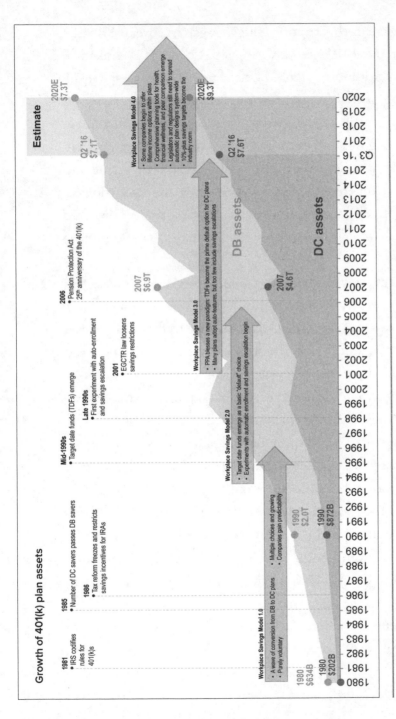

FIGURE 3.3 The evolution of workplace savings in America, 1980–2020

Investment Company Institute. 2016. "The U.S. Retirement Market, Third Quarter 2016." www.ici.org/research/stats. Collins, Sean, Sarah Holden, James Duvall, and Elena Barone Chism. 2016. "The Economics of Providing 401(k) Plans: Services, Fees, and Expenses, 2015." ICI Research Perspective 22, no. 4 (July). Available at www.ici.org/pdf/per22-04.pdf. Source: Investment Company Institute, Washington, DC. Cerulli Associates: The Cerulli Report: Global Markets 2016: Growth Through Reform and Innovation—Exhibit 2.26; and Putnam estimates.

CHAPTER 4

THE PENSION PROTECTION ACT OF 2006: 401(K) SAVINGS BECOMES A SYSTEM

Do what you can, where you are,
with what you have.
—TEDDY ROOSEVELT

To understand how the Pension Protection Act of 2006 changed key practices in retirement savings, we should step back a moment to first look at the investment theory that helped to drive these changes.

Modern Portfolio Theory

Modern portfolio theory (MPT), the master doctrine behind most of today's asset management practice, was born in the early 1950s with the publication of a seminal paper, "Portfolio Selection," in the *Journal of Finance*, written by a then-unknown analyst named Harry Markowitz. The paper proved to be one of the most influential financial monographs of all time. In a nutshell, MPT set out a theoretical framework for the construction of portfolios built along what Markowitz called an "efficient frontier" that maximizes a portfolio's returns at any given level of risk.

MPT suggests that wise risk management requires a holistic view of how all elements in any given portfolio (stocks, bonds, derivatives, and other assets) perform in concert. Markowitz's theory also made it conventional wisdom that healthy returns depend on consciously engaging risk over time. MPT convinced pension funds in particular that stock market volatility tends to smooth out in the long run, thus dampening the impact of the often sharp downturns that are bound to occur over any long-term investment horizon.

In the decades since Markowitz's great insight, mutual fund managers and DB pension fund trustees made excellent use of MPT's tool kit. Sophisticated pension plan management became almost routine. Financial professionals came to make nearly all fund decisions. Companies that sponsored DB workplace savings plans bore all the risk. And since the life of pension funds is far longer than the life expectancies of individual workers, that investment risk was spread across decades.

Plan sponsors and their fund managers were better able to navigate through short-term market ups and downs and focus on long-term investment growth and compounding. The lucky minority of workers who enjoyed access to defined benefit pensions had few, if any, choices to make. All they needed to do was hold their jobs as long as possible and make plans for a long retirement near their beach or golf course of choice.

Many of the same key insights—simplicity, diversification, mitigation of risk—could well have been applied as 401(k) plans and other defined contribution systems emerged in the 1980s. But when DC plans first came on the scene, it was not obvious that they needed to incorporate sophisticated financial theories like MPT in their designs. After all, the new DC plans were initially used to top off traditional pensions, usually for highly paid senior managers, many of them experienced investors looking for choice and comfortable with risk.

Explosive Growth of Defined Contribution Plans

But DC assets under management expanded more dramatically and the plans moved to the center of retirement finance much faster than anyone anticipated. When ERISA became law in the mid-1970s, there were 2.4 employees in traditional pension plans for every employee in the newly emerging DC plans. But as ERISA made the provision of traditional pensions more burdensome and expensive, many more companies began to see the potential for DC plans to take a more prominent role, or even to replace traditional pension plans.

The take-up of DC plans was explosive. In just five years, from 1985 to 1990, workplace 401(k) plans rose from an aggregate value of $427 billion to $712 billion according to the Investment Company Institute (ICI)—compound growth of about 12 percent a year. Over the next 15 years, from 1990 to 2005, defined contribution plans of all types more than tripled from $900 billion to $3 trillion.

As early as 1983, the number of American workers in DC plans had surpassed those in DB plans. By 1997, DC assets under management surpassed those of DB plans (never to return), and by 2004, DC participants outnumbered those in DB plans by 2.5:1, a complete inversion of the ratio of 30 years prior.

Workplace Savings 1.0

These early years of the defined contribution savings boom mark a phase in their evolution that we can call Workplace Savings 1.0. This initial flurry of DC plan growth came against the backdrop of a long, powerful bull market in stocks that began in 1982. It was marked by a competitive rush to offer workplace savers an ever-expanding menu of investment choices—often, perhaps, too broad a menu. Along the way, risk and responsibility for investment choices shifted steadily away from companies and pension professionals to the workers themselves.

In traditional pension plans, virtually all critical decisions such as whether or not to save, the level of savings, investment selection, asset allocation, and calculations of the level of income needed to maintain lifestyle in retirement were made by pension experts employed by defined benefit plan sponsors and their service providers.

By contrast, workplace savers in the defined contribution plans were left entirely to their own devices, backed up by only limited investment information and minimal guidance provided by most plan sponsors. The three most critical decisions of retirement savings—when to begin saving, how much to save, and how to allocate their assets—were left to individuals with little or no financial expertise.

Little wonder that many of these workers, faced with a host of investment choices and the complex challenge of estimating retirement income needs, made less than perfect choices. Many fell into one of more of these strategic pitfalls:

- Excessive risk concentration—either by overcommitting to company stock or choosing a 100 percent "risk-on" all-stock portfolio.
- Market timing—chasing after high returns or panic selling into downturns.
- Extreme risk aversion—wholly committing to low-risk, low-return money market funds that couldn't earn enough to supply robust retirement income.

In retirement, some of these early DC plan investors could do little better than adopt best-guess strategies for converting their accumulated assets into income—either immediately annuitizing, or spending down their savings as needed and hoping not to drain their savings too soon.

In this early phase of the defined contribution industry, the combination of breakneck growth and substandard execution was historically unique. Never before had millions of ordinary workers been able to engage in such a robust wages-to-wealth mechanism, and with such unfettered freedom to make predictable investment mistakes. As early as the mid-1980s, it was becoming obvious that the amateur asset allocators investing in 401(k)s and similar plans were often falling short of their goals.

Since DC plans, unlike most traditional pensions, were purely voluntary, many workers simply never took the affirmative step of signing up to save in the first place. Others saved too little, made overly risky or overly cautious investment allocations, or cashed out of their plans when they changed jobs instead of staying invested for the long haul by moving those funds to an IRA or their new employer's plan.

A sharp irony underlying the era of Workplace Savings 1.0 was that many employers were in fact concerned that shifting investment risk to workers might be less than ideal. But they hesitated to either limit investment choices or offer detailed financial advice for fear of exposing themselves to legal liability.

Increasingly, though, many companies did make serious efforts to offer their workers some investment guidance. In fact, by the 1990s America's DC plan sponsors were investing hundreds of millions of dollars a year nationally in "C&E"—communications and education. Brochures, websites, investment seminars, and other efforts to acquaint workers with basic concepts such as diversification and dollar-cost averaging abounded. These costly communications efforts did produce at the margin. But none moved the needle radically in terms of lifting participation, savings rates, or overall results.

More significantly, also during the mid-1990s, some forward-thinking plan sponsors began experimenting with plan designs that would do far more to engage workers. These ideas centered on the then-radical concept of "automaticity" or "negative election"—automatic enrollment in a savings plan with the ability to opt out. Automatic savings escalation from an initially low rate was another similarly radical idea. So was helping to improve workers' investment allocations through structured investment offerings—"default" investment strategies that workers would be guided to if they made no specific choices among plan options on their own.

These first stirrings of what we will call Workplace Savings 2.0 plan designs began in the 1990s. They thus coincided, fortuitously, with rising academic interest in DC plans as a system, and fresh research into the factors that drive and shape workplace savers' choices and behaviors.

Workplace Savings 2.0:
The Influence of Behavioral Finance

Looking back, it's not surprising that the surge in DC plan formation from the late 1980s on was powerful enough to attract serious attention from academic theorists interested in labor and retirement economics.

As a few thousand pension funds were rapidly being replaced by millions of individual investment portfolios, a whole new and unproven system of retirement savings seemed to many financial theorists to be emerging. So was a whole new school of behavioral economics, which blended economics and finance with psychological and even sociological approaches to analyze the often irrational forces that motivate individuals' decision making.

Conventional economics had long relied on the strange notion that economic actors are cool, rational decision makers (the so-called *Homo economicus*). Like the ultra-logical Mr. Spock of *Star Trek*, economic man supposedly employs pure reason and self-interest to weigh choices among incentives, risks, financial goals, and strategies.

But as the new breed of behavioral economists soon learned from research on actual workplace plans and savers, average workers bore little resemblance to that idealized fantasy. Like most human beings, workplace savers were, are, and always will be complex, flawed, and emotionally driven, and poorly prepared to make fundamental decisions about their long-term financial welfare without some expert guidance.

By the mid-1990s, forward-thinking companies understood this and recognized an urgent need for guidelines and guardrails to help their workers make better decisions for their defined contribution savings. So the companies began to collaborate with leading behavioral finance researchers. Several exciting avenues of inquiry and insight quickly emerged. Here are some of their findings:

- Individual investors systematically demonstrate overconfidence in their investment decision making.
- They value the present at the expense of the future, and commonly exhibit "framing" bias, which is a tendency to make financial decisions in response to the ways the options are presented.
- They are extremely loss-averse.
- Most people are ill equipped, even unable, to handle the complex life-cycle analysis needed to plan for lifetime income and to anticipate lifetime earnings, asset returns, tax rates, likely family/health status, and longevity.

- Faced with too many investment options, many investors experience choice overload and disengage, either by minimizing their deferrals, choosing low-return money market investments, or simply not enrolling.
- Inertia, the tendency to stay on any given course once it is chosen, may well be the most powerful force in retirement savings behavior. Inertia can work for or against savers' best interests depending on which choices they are "nudged" to make to begin with.
- Financial education, while laudable, usually does little to move the needle on savings. Awareness alone, absent action, won't materially improve outcomes.
- Not least, studies showed that since savings rates tend to rise with income and age, purely voluntary workplace savings plans disproportionately benefit more highly compensated employees who are more able to save disposable income.

Most important, the research revealed an array of highly positive possibilities involving automaticity and choice architecture, elements of workplace savings plan design that could be used to default workers into optimal behaviors, while still allowing them to opt out if they choose to.

When workers are not automatically enrolled in savings plans, their default decision is too often to save nothing. And even intensive communications and education programs rarely lifted participation in workplace savings much over 60 percent. But early experiments with automatic enrollment found that it could often raise participation rates from 60 percent to over 90 percent because few workers, once engaged, chose to make the deliberate decision to opt out.

Financial Literacy Versus Plan Design

It should not be surprising to see the multiple errors to which ordinary workplace savers are prone. Even veteran investment professionals, after all, succumb to strong emotions at times. And very few of the first generation of worker-investors in DC plans had any experience in finance, certainly not in the arcane arts of asset allocation, mean variance optimization, Monte Carlo simulation, or probabilistic scenario analysis.

Many 401(k) savers thus employed naive or what finance professionals term "1/N" allocations. If offered five investment options, for example a value fund, a growth fund, a bond fund, a balanced fund, and a money market fund, many workers would simply divide their allocation by five, directing 20 percent of their savings into each of the options. When faced with too many options—15, 20, or even more choices had become common in many plans by the 1990s—many workplace savers simply froze, or stowed their investments in money market funds earning minuscule returns.

Forward-thinking planners, fortified by new academic insights, began to think very differently about how to help people save effectively. Realizing that tax incentives, investor education, and other reason-based incentives weren't cutting it, the retirement savings industry began to suspect that workplace plan design itself—the way that workers' investment choices are framed—could do much more to improve outcomes than any amount of spending on participant communications and education. No matter how worthy financial literacy and investor education programs may be, there's no reason to think they will ever turn Americans into a nation of Warren Buffets.

The Birth of Target Date Funds

Parallel to creative research being undertaken in the area of plan design in the early 1990s, Wells Fargo's investment arm began offering a brilliantly intuitive new financial product, target date funds (TDFs). Also known as life-cycle funds, TDFs are mutual funds that blend the higher risks and returns of stocks with lower-risk, lower-return bonds, changing that allocation over time up to, and sometimes beyond, a specific target date often decades into the future.

This single innovation dramatically simplified decision making for retirement savers in workplace plans since all they would need to calculate was their own desired retirement date—say, 2040—and pick a fund with that target date. Over the years, the fund's managers would steadily shift the investments in the fund along a "glide path" from higher- to lower-risk assets as the fund's target date neared.

TDFs thus enabled savers to take higher risk and seek higher returns from stocks when they still had many years to recover from any market slumps. They were then guided steadily to less risky TDFs offered as their proposed retirement date neared. In essence, this was one-stop shopping for a dynamic lifelong investment strategy with advice and guidance built right into the product itself.

The stars were aligning. TDFs were superbly suited to defined contribution workplace savings plans. The late 1990s saw these two innovations, TDFs and efficient DC retirement savings plans, surge along with an historic stock market boom. Over that decade, the Dow Average tripled while the technology-heavy NASDAQ surged by 800 percent.

Riding the wave, total U.S. defined contribution savings expanded by 15 percent a year from 1990 to 1995 to top $1.3 trillion at mid-decade. These massive flows to workplace savings made it clear that DC plans were here to stay, and would soon become the nation's primary source of future retirement income.

The bold experiments underway in behavioral economics, together with solution-seeking innovations like target date funds and experiments in automated plan design by forward-thinking plan sponsors, also made it clear that a new paradigm for retirement savings in America was struggling to be born.

Workplace Savings 1.0 had been purely voluntary, heavily dependent on communications and education, and offering multiple choices and very limited guidance and planning. Most default options guided participants to supposedly safe stable value and money market funds, which could never grow enough to fund a comfortable retirement.

This voluntary structure required participants to make the right call several times—to participate, to save the maximum allowed by law, to diversify, and to rebalance as markets evolved and as they got older. This complex decision-making structure for retirement savings made it hard for workers to succeed and easy for them to fail.

The Workplace Savings 2.0 plan designs emerging by the late 1990s were better attuned to behavioral solutions. New concepts like "choice architecture" and "nudge" economics aimed to make it easier for workers to make the right choices. In fact, automatic plans would guide workers who made no choices at all into participating (unless they opted out), saving more over time, and investing in target-date solutions that would manage risks and returns for them all the way to their retirement dates.

Just by doing nothing, such workers could let profession-ally designed defaults do the flying for them, just as computer algorithms do for jumbo jets. Such plan designs would make retirement savings success easy and failure hard.

While some of the most progressive employers were exper-imenting with these novel autopilot ideas, most plan sponsors were hesitant to adopt them for fear that they or their share-holders might be subject to serious legal liability. A significantly better form of retirement savings was trying to be born, but it needed regulatory support and a firmer legal foundation and protection. In 2006, plan sponsors and participants finally got that major boost from Washington.

The PPA Codifies Behavioral Finance

When President George W. Bush signed the Pension Protection Act (PPA) into law in August 2006, it was the most substantial pension reform legislation since ERISA over 30 years earlier. The PPA gave legal blessing to the autopilot innovations that progressive plan sponsors had been experimenting with for years. It also validated the insights and solutions advanced by behavioral economists who had worked on retirement savings. Specifically:

- The PPA allowed for automatic enrollment of plan partici-pants but allowed for an opt-out should they decide not to participate.
- The law acknowledged the significance of employer contribu-tions to employee accounts, whether as a match to employees'

71

contributions or freely given. (A few employers actually do put money in a worker's plan even if the worker doesn't.)

- The automatic escalation of participant contributions was provided for, beginning at a level of 3 percent and escalating annually until it reached 6 percent, with an upper limit of 10 percent. Additional contributions could be made through employee election.

- The law also took an important step toward improving asset allocation by approving three qualified default investment alternatives (QDIAs): target date funds, balanced funds, and professionally managed accounts.

By green-lighting automaticity, the law sought to nudge employees into initiating and expanding their retirement savings. It also gave an important assist to employers: safe harbor from annual nondiscrimination testing for workplace plans that adopted automatic enrollment and savings escalation. Nondiscrimination testing is an expensive, cumbersome process by which employers must demonstrate that the tax benefits of their plans do not unfairly accrue to highly compensated employees. The safe harbor component of the PPA thus represented an effective endorsement of the key plan design features of Workplace Savings 2.0.

Legislative Validation and Market Consensus

PPA was an outstanding and all-too-rare example of something we need more of in America: well-grounded, evidence-based reform drawing on both academic analysis and real-world market experience. Rather than cooking up a master plan and foisting it on the market, Congress let the market and academic researchers take the lead and prove out concepts in the real world. Then they granted legal and regulatory imprimatur to a new line of thinking that had emerged over two decades of financial evolution. With the Pension Protection Act of 2006, Congress effectively endorsed a series of creative innovations that had evolved through the interplay of competitive market forces.

Remarkably, academics, practitioners, regulators, and elected representatives got it right. They recognized that DC plans were well on their way to becoming America's prime retirement savings vehicle. And they gave these plans permission to adopt a dramatically improved set of design ideas that would enable them to do a much better job helping millions of American workers secure robust, reliable incomes for life. With the PPA enacted, 401(k)s, which began as just a supplemental add-on benefit for top executives, took a huge step toward becoming the primary private savings element in America's national retirement system.

Amid our era of poisonous political partisanship, it's worth recalling that the PPA was a broadly bipartisan achievement. Sponsored by John Boehner, Republican representative for Ohio's 8th Congressional district, it passed the House of Representatives by a vote of 279 to 131, including 76 votes from Democrats. In the Senate, it drew even stronger, overwhelming support: 93 to 5, with 52 Republicans, 40 Democrats, and one Independent voting "yea."

PPA seemed important at the time. With a decade's hindsight, it seems like a critical inflection point in the history of

American finance. In almost every respect—enrollment, deferral savings including escalation, and asset allocation—it has been very good news for all concerned.

The Pioneers of Behavioral Economics

Over the decades of my career, the financial services industry has spent billions on education, communications, and marketing programs in furtherance of "financial literacy." But despite years of striving to empower retirement savers, we have little to show for it. No amount of knowledge, motivation, and encouragement seems to have moved the retirement savings needle. It isn't that our efforts didn't add value; in fact, they were insightful, accurate, and wise. The problem was that we were speaking to a customer who didn't exist.

Modern economic theory was developed based on the rational, objective decision-making capabilities of a mythical *Homo economicus*, a disinterested, coldly rational creature who can be trusted to absorb information, quantify risk, optimize investment strategies, and take methodical action.

But the truth is that most real-world retirement savers cannot process the complex data, variables, and options required of the investment process. Rather, they operate within the limitations of what economists called "bounded rationality"—with their decisions limited by their access to information, cognitive abilities, and time.

But as luck would have it, just as the emerging retirement savings eras of Workplace Savings 1.0 and 2.0 arose, a new breed of economists were incorporating social, psychological, and emotional factors into the accelerating field of behavioral economics (and its subset, behavioral finance). Their timing was perfect. American workers, newly responsible for saving and managing their investments, had been floundering in their attempt to deal with multiyear investment horizons and make decisions that were complex, emotional, and prone to miscalculations.

The behavioral economists riding to the rescue had developed several techniques for decision framing and choice architecture that had been proven in academia and in the marketplace and were then incorporated into the Pension Protection Act in 2006, dramatically expanding automaticity and incorporating retirement savings best practices.

- **Brigitte C. Madrian and Dennis F. Shea.** Their early impactful 2001 paper, "The Power of Suggestion: Inertia in 401(k) Participation and Savings Behavior," revealed that automatic enrollment significantly increased 401(k) participation, and that a substantial portion of 401(k) participants hired under automatic enrollment had left their default contribution rates and fund allocations unchanged indefinitely.

- **Richard H. Thaler and Cass R. Sunstein.** Their remarkable book, *Nudge*, explained behavioral economics to the world in a way no other book had before. For retirement savers, they strongly advocated automatic enrollment, escalation, and allocation, sparing savers conscious decision making (or anxiety) in the process.

- **Dan Ariely.** Professor Dan Ariely, author of *Predictably Irrational* and *The Upside of Irrationality*, has mapped the emotional underpinning of human decision making and concluded that we are neither coldly rational nor rigorously quantitative when facing critical choices. As with other behavioral economists, we are able to infer from his work that automaticity, guardrails, and other structures of choice architecture facilitate decision making and help avoid emotional missteps.

- **Shlomo Benartzi and Roger Lewin.** In their books *Thinking Smarter* and *Save More Tomorrow*, they suggested that investors tend to overthink their retirement planning, cluttering the process with short-term, narrowly informed decisions. They noted that fully one-third of Americans with access to workplace savings chose not to participate and those who did tended to save too little and make unwise investment decisions.

- **Daniel Kahneman.** In his book *Thinking, Fast and Slow*, the Princeton psychologist and Nobel Prize winner identified the corrosive financial consequences of optimism, overconfidence, and snap judgments driven by emotion and impulse. He noted that investors had an exaggerated bias against loss and incorrectly believed that the future could be rendered predictable.

- **William Gale, Mark Iwry, David John, and Lina Walker.** While not actually behavioral economists, this remarkable team of retirement policy experts developed their book *Automatic* squarely on the foundation of

behavioral finance, offering up a comprehensive proposal for Automatic IRAs that, while not yet enacted
into federal law, has inspired emerging state-sponsored
private retirement savings around the country.

Thanks to behavioral economics, investors are ben-
efiting from default enrollments with opt-outs, decision
trees, and asset allocation algorithms that promise to
bring retirement savings up to date with fields such as
data management and networking, telecommunications, healthcare, and transportation, where automated,
default decision making has led to measurably superior
outcomes.

The Power of Automaticity

There is no more powerful demonstration of the sheer
impact on people's decision making of automatic enrollment (or "negative election" as economists call it) than a
classic article in *Science* magazine from November 2003,
"Do Defaults Save Lives?" by Eric Johnson and Daniel
Goldstein. The authors compared the relative willingness
of citizens of 11 European countries to become organ
donors, a decision that can and does save the lives of
fellow citizens.

Four of the nations surveyed rely on purely voluntary
sign-ups by their citizens and devote major resources to
encourage them to do so. But since signing up to donate
in these countries requires making a positive choice,

the most successful program, in the Netherlands, convinced only 27.5 percent of Dutch citizens to volunteer. By contrast, seven other nations sign up all their citizens as donors automatically, unless they make the "negative election" to opt out.

Sweden, the *least* successful of these automatic donor nations, still finds that over 85 percent of citizens remain organ donors. Only 14 percent of Swedes deliberately choose to opt out. The most striking single contrast is between Germany's voluntary opt-in model and neighboring Austria's negative election, opt-out system. People in both nations speak German, enjoy beer, and waltz to Mozart. But their organ donation rates are radically different—just 12 percent in Germany versus 99.98 percent in Austria (Figure 4.1).

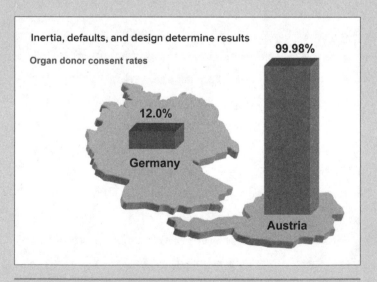

FIGURE 4.1 The power of auto-enrollment

Source: sciencemag.org, vol. 302, November 21, 2003.

There's no better demonstration of the impact of behavioral "nudges," "decision framing," or the sheer power of inertia. All of our experience with automatic enrollment and savings escalation programs in U.S. workplace plans confirms the key insight here: Automaticity is critical to successful plan design. Indeed, automaticity should be the standard for the retirement industry. While still preserving the freedom to opt out, it turns inertia into a positive force for workplace savers' benefit.

CHAPTER 5

WORKPLACE SAVINGS 3.0: FINDING THE KEYS TO RETIREMENT READINESS

*Whether you think you can or you
think you can't, you're right.*
—**HENRY FORD**

The Pension Protection Act of 2006 actually worked better than many of us had expected. By offering official legislative and regulatory support for a series of best practices such as auto-enrollment or automatic savings escalation, the law significantly speeded the uptake of powerful, effective ideas that were already evolving in the retirement markets.

More importantly, its passage marked the moment when Congress and leading national policy makers began to treat workplace plans like the 401(k) as America's primary retirement income source of the future. The new law's key provisions, in turn, enabled those plans to take huge strides toward realizing their full potential.

Ten years later, the passage of the PPA looks increasingly like a transformative event. We have seen a host of dramatic, positive changes sweep across America's workplace savings system. We have effectively proven a model for accumulating retirement assets. We have set many millions of workers on track to solve the challenge of reliably replacing their full work-life incomes for the rest of their days. We've taken great steps forward.

But as we will see, this success is still only partial and strictly limited to the accumulation side of retirement policy. We still need to provide workplace savings plans for tens of millions of workers who lack any payroll savings plan on the job. We even have a lot of work ahead to spread the best practices that PPA endorsed to all existing workplace plans. And the question of solving the distribution side of retirement policy—converting lifetime savings to reliable lifelong income—is a far thornier problem that we have just started to address.

Still, taking a quick look at how far we've come in the 10 years since the PPA's passage should give us hope that we can, and will, solve these unmet challenges. After all, in the decade since the PPA, total U.S. workplace and IRA retirement savings have grown by a solid 6 percent per year (net of redemptions) despite the 2008–2009 global market crisis, ongoing financial stresses, and near-zero interest rates worldwide.

Across many metrics, from plan enrollment to guided investment choices to costs and fees, workplace savings plans have steadily improved. Here are just some of the changes we've

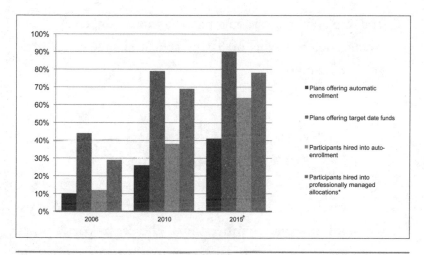

FIGURE 5.1 Highlights of "How America Saves 2016"—impact of PPA participant account management

Source: ©The Vanguard Group, Inc., 2016, used with permission.

seen in the PPA's first decade, summed up in the Vanguard Group's excellent annual survey, "How America Saves 2016" (Figure 5.1).

- In 2006, only 12 percent of new employees had access to plans that automatically enrolled them. Today 63 percent of new hires are in plans that use automatic enrollment.
- In 2006, only 10 percent of plans offered auto-enrollment; today that number is 41 percent.
- In 2006, only 12 percent of plan participants were hired by companies whose plans offered professionally managed asset allocation strategies (target date or life-cycle funds, balanced funds, or managed accounts); today that number is 48 percent, and projected to be 68 percent by 2020.
- In 2006, only 43 percent of plans offered life-cycle funds; today that number is 90 percent.

- Today, plan participation rates are a robust 78 percent, with average deferral rates of 6.8 percent and median deferral rates of 5.9 percent.

Participant Contribution and Asset Allocation

These positive trends in basic plan design have been accompanied by significantly better investment choices by participants, often guided by their use of the plans' own default investment options, blessed and sanctioned by the PPA.

Workplace savings plans that at the outset of the 401(k) era offered multiple, seemingly random investment options have since adopted much more effective strategies like target date funds or managed accounts that embed advice into the funds' design and aim specifically to mitigate risk as retirement approaches.

"How America Saves" also notes real improvements in workplace savers' asset allocation:

- In 2006, investors had 15 percent of their allocations in cash; by 2015, this had been reduced to 7 percent.
- In 2006, plan savers held fully 9 percent of their retirement savings in company stock; today, that share has dropped to 4 percent.
- Contributions to target date funds have exploded, rising from just 4 percent of workplace plan contributions in 2006 to 46 percent by 2015, a rise of over 1,000 percent (Figure 5.2).

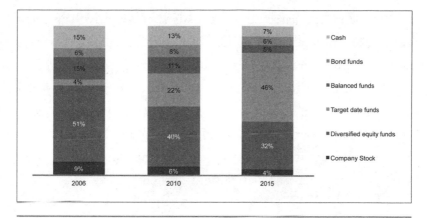

FIGURE 5.2 Highlights of "How America Saves 2016"—impact of PPA plan contribution allocation summary

Source: ©The Vanguard Group, Inc., 2016, used with permission.

One fundamental insight we can derive from seeing the impact of the auto-features endorsed by the PPA is that plan design itself determines both workplace savers' choices and their results. What economists call framing or choice architecture heavily influences the choices that real working people actually make. So establishing the right framework for automatic decision making and providing guidance to well-designed default investment strategies can dramatically improve people's chances of success.

Automatic plan design can, in fact, make success easy and failure hard.

That's because inertia is the strongest single factor in workers' saving behavior. It is near-universal. And smart plan design can make this force work for savers, and not against them.

Just a few years after the PPA gave automatic enrollment formal approval, for example, the percentage of plan sponsors adopting auto-enrollment for their workers more than tripled.

What their experience now tells us is that roughly 90 percent of people who are auto-enrolled in workplace savings plans go with the flow and stay in; less than 10 percent opt out.

That kind of lift in workers' participation rates vastly outpaces the gains in enrollment that companies spent millions of dollars to achieve through communications and investor education. And it requires major changes by plan sponsors who make the choice to go full auto in designing their plans.

Workplace Plan Design and Investor Education

With the passage of the PPA, policy makers and plan sponsors recognized the sheer power of plan design, structure, and the framing of choices in shaping participants' results. Automatic enrollment, savings escalation, and guidance into life-cycle or balanced fund defaults have since been shown to have much more impact on the basic variables of plan participation, savings rates, and investment choices than traditional communications and education efforts ever did—at far lower cost.

That doesn't mean that investor education and financial literacy programs are without value. But they do need to change to better serve participants' needs in an automatic plan environment. A fair analogy between plan structure and education might be a comparison to the role of driver education in highway safety.

No one would question the value of both classroom instruction and hands-on tutoring in enabling new drivers to take to the road safely. But few would disagree that driver safety is even more dramatically improved by structural elements such as airbags, seat belts, antilock brakes, and crush-resistant passenger compartments. While some drivers might want to know something about how cars actually work, most people only want to know how to drive successfully. They don't care at all about the chemistry of Internal combustion, metallurgy, or automotive electronics. Similarly, few retirement savers know or care about the arcane details of portfolio construction or asset management.

So adopting an automatic plan design segments a workforce into several different groups whose educational needs vary dramatically. Most workers, and surely a majority of younger ones, have little or no interest in investments, markets, or the economy. They will follow the cues created for them in a plan's basic recommendations or its defaults. They need little more than regular information explaining the advantages offered by a plan's defaults, and guidance that urges them to stay the course and not lock in losses during periods of market turbulence.

A small minority of employees, typically about 10 percent, will choose to save nothing and opt out entirely. These workers need targeted educational outreach to change their minds, plus automatic annual reenrollment that requires them to make another opt-out choice every year. If and when they are finally enrolled, inertia can work for and not against them as their savings grow.

Another significant share of the employee population, the so-called "self-directed investors," want to actively manage their own investment choices. These participants will likely include higher-paid, better-educated workers. They need access to robust web services, regular communications on investments, in-house seminars on plan options, and access to paid professional advice as an option.

Going full-auto in plan design thus requires a carefully targeted educational effort. The good news for plan sponsors is that such a program may actually be less expensive for them and more effective because it more fully addresses each group's needs.

Gains, Flaws, and Shortfalls

The data from PPA's first decade show that the most striking gains in saving for retirement are secured by the least prepared segment of the workforce. The biggest beneficiaries of our evolving full auto workplace plan system are younger and less-well-paid employees, provided they have access to an auto-enrolled plan.

In an increasingly automated workplace savings system, younger workers' income replacement rates stand to jump far more dramatically in the years to come than those of older, higher-paid employees, many of whom have far less than a full career's exposure to 401(k)-type savings and may not have had the time horizon to benefit from features like automatic savings escalation.

One unintended, though perhaps predictable, consequence of the PPA has been a different rate of adoption of auto-features between large and small plans. In financial services, as with most industries in a market economy, scale matters. So large plans can drive better terms from service providers, give their employees more generous incentives and matches, and dedicate more resources to ensuring that workers save and escalate their savings over time. We will need to find ways to encourage—and incent—more small businesses to provide plans and make them fully automatic.

But even as we celebrate the emergence of the full auto vision, it is important to recognize that serious errors have been made by far too many plan designers in the post-PPA era.

The 3 Percent Glitch

The most serious error of too many plan designers, by far, is their tendency to offer initial savings deferral rates of 3 percent or even less, without any provision for automatically raising them. This single bureaucratic miscue, call it "the 3 percent glitch," has had the perverse effect of taking a brilliant idea, automaticity, and causing it to actually undermine workers' own best interests.

The origin of this misbegotten practice stems from the mention of 3 percent as a good starting point for workplace plans' savings rates in one of the Treasury Department rulings in the late 1990s that authorized companies to adopt auto-enrollment. Too many plan sponsors took the mere mention of 3 percent savings rates as a guideline to follow, not just a place to start. Talk about unintended consequences!

Just last year, a decade after PPA's passage, T. Rowe Price reported that over 38 percent of the plans they serve still enroll workers at an initial savings rate of just 3 percent. That's better than nothing, of course. But the problem is that far too many workers auto-enrolled at 3 percent savings rates just stay there, obeying the most powerful force in retirement policy: inertia. That's why the savings rates in auto-enrolled plans can actually be lower than those found in purely voluntary plans, where workers typically sign up to save 5 percent or more.

Some academics have perversely seized on this anomaly to claim that auto-enrollment itself is somehow inferior to purely voluntary plans. But the problem is not automaticity itself, it is the failure of some plan sponsors to adopt a fully automatic plan design package, including automatic savings escalation and guidance to dynamic default investments that automatically reduce the level of risk as retirement approaches, without workers having to make that decision on their own.

The 3 percent glitch, in other words, is caused by too little use of automatic plan design features, not too much. And there's no doubt that low savings levels, like overly conservative investment choices, can have a corrosive long-term impact on retirement preparation. The truth is that we don't serve anyone well by allowing them to believe that saving 3 percent or 5 percent or even 7 percent will be enough to enable them to finance a retirement income lasting 20 or 30 years or more.

For workers to take full advantage of market-based retirement savings, it is also critical to take age-appropriate levels of risk. Socking away savings in low-risk, low-return money market funds once did seem like a safe strategy for workplace savings plan design. Many first-generation 401(k) plans chose money market funds as a default. Today, we know better. Far from being safe, such strategies can be very dangerous if the goal is financing lifelong income.

In an age of persistently low interest rates, most "safe" investments virtually guarantee savings shortfalls over a long-term investment horizon. Even retirees need some investments that stand a chance of beating inflation. Retirement savers are all but obliged to invest some share of their savings in riskier assets like stocks. These may, indeed, be more volatile. But equities offer at least the chance of real long-term wealth appreciation. The opportunity costs of not owning them usually outweigh their risks.

Income Replacement: The Ratio That Defines Retirement Success

The ultimate goal of workplace savings, and the best measure of any retirement savings plan or system's success, is its ability to amass enough wealth to ensure reliable income for life. So the best measure of retirement readiness shouldn't focus on any absolute number, but on the income that retirement savings can generate, expressed as a percentage of what retirees earned while working.

Retirement planners call this the replacement ratio, which is calculated by simply dividing a retiree's income by what he or she earned prior to retirement. For example, if a retiree who used to earn $100,000 a year is able to draw $50,000 a year in Social Security and private retirement income after retiring, then the replacement ratio is 50 percent.

There is no consensus among advisors, planners, or the retirement services industry on what the ideal replacement ratio is and whether workers should aim for 60 percent, 80 percent, or more. The answer varies widely among individuals, families, and different regions of the country. Perhaps the only consensus is that more is more, while anything close to or over 100 percent would be an unquestionable win, perhaps even a bit of an overshoot.

Empower Retirement's Lifetime Income Score (LIS)

That's why first Putnam Investments and now Empower Retirement, both companies that I lead, set out in 2010 to quantify working Americans' ability to replace their income in retirement. We asked our research colleagues at Brightwork Partners to take account of all sources future retirees can draw on: Social Security, traditional pensions, workplace savings plans like 401(k)s, savings, insurance, home equity, and even ownership shares in a business.

We have since assessed the total assets of more than 4,000 working Americans aged 18 to 65 every year with a sample weighted to match U.S. census parameters. The resulting Lifetime Income Survey provides one of the most comprehensive assessments of potential retirement readiness in the country.

What's more, we can also drill down into the LIS survey data to see how different subsets of workers are progressing toward the goal of income replacement. The survey thus gives us both a snapshot of where we stand 11 years after the

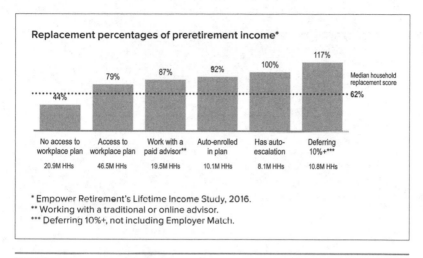

Replacement percentages of preretirement income*

No access to workplace plan	Access to workplace plan	Work with a paid advisor**	Auto-enrolled in plan	Has auto-escalation	Deferring 10%+***
44%	79%	87%	92%	100%	117%
20.9M HHs	46.5M HHs	19.5M HHs	10.1M HHs	8.1M HHs	10.8M HHs

Median household replacement score 62%

* Empower Retirement's Lifetime Income Study, 2016.
** Working with a traditional or online advisor.
*** Deferring 10%+, not including Employer Match.

FIGURE 5.3 Where we are now: six states of retirement readiness in America

Source: Empower Retirement LIS VI.

PPA's passage, and a guide to policy moves the country can make to radically improve all Americans' prospects for retirement success.

The sixth edition of the Lifetime Income Score Research, published in April 2016, found that, at the median, working Americans are on track overall to replace 62 percent of their working life income once they retire. (Median, of course, means that half the population will be able to replace more than 62 percent, while half the people will be able to replace less.) The survey also discloses major differences in replacement rates among different groups of workers. In effect, it gives us an x-ray of a very clear hierarchy of best practices in workplace plan design that help increase retirement readiness. Let's look first at the overall picture, and then tease out some critical variables. Figure 5.3 gives an overall view of how American households

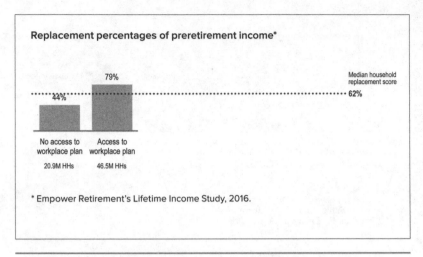

Replacement percentages of preretirement income*

79%

44%

Median household
replacement score

62%

No access to
workplace plan
20.9M HHs

Access to
workplace plan
46.5M HHs

* Empower Retirement's Lifetime Income Study, 2016.

FIGURE 5.4   Why closing the "coverage gap" is so vital

Source: Empower Retirement LIS VI.

are faring in terms of retirement readiness a decade after the Pension Protection Act of 2006.

A look at Figure 5.4 shows that lack of access itself is the system's single most acute shortfall, with nearly 21 million households having no savings plan at work. These workers are on track to replace just 44 percent of their preretirement income, even including Social Security. In fact, having access to some form of workplace payroll deduction lifts prospective replacement ratios by fully 35 percent—from 44 percent to 79 percent, the single biggest leap in this series.

Those with no workplace savings plan—42 million of our fellow Americans—are likely to face a sharp drop in living standards in retirement, perhaps outright poverty. Acting to close this coverage gap is the single most powerful move we could make to raise savings and improve retirement readiness in

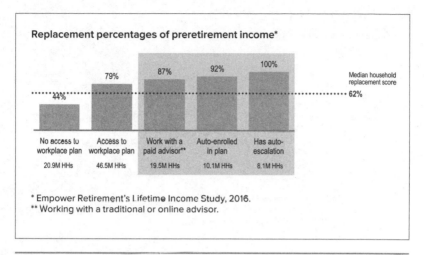

Replacement percentages of preretirement income*

No access to workplace plan	Access to workplace plan	Work with a paid advisor**	Auto-enrolled in plan	Has auto-escalation
44%	79%	87%	92%	100%
20.9M HHs	46.5M HHs	19.5M HHs	10.1M HHs	8.1M HHs

Median household replacement score 62%

* Empower Retirement's Lifetime Income Study, 2016.
** Working with a traditional or online advisor.

FIGURE 5.5 Three key enhancements to workplace plan design

Source: Empower Retirement LIS VI.

America. The coverage gap effectively defines the crossroads of wise savings policy and basic decency.

A series of other key enhancements to workplace savings plan design do much to further lift workers' prospects of full retirement readiness. Having access to a paid financial advisor lifts income replacement to a median level of 87 percent (Figure 5.5). (See box, "The Value of Advice.") Workers in plans that automatically enroll them and automatically escalate their savings from the initial rate are on track to secure 92 percent and 100 percent replacement rates respectively. Even bearing in mind that these are median results, they are impressive gains, driven very clearly by workplace savings plan design itself.

The most powerful variable of all is simple: More is more. Workers in plans who have achieved savings rates of 10 percent or more are on track at the median to replace fully 117 percent of their work-life income. This is success by any reasonable

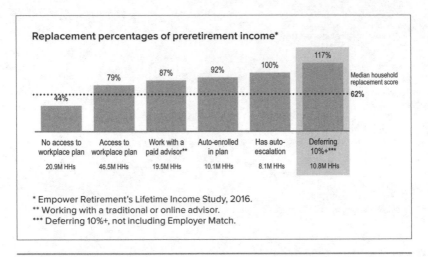

FIGURE 5.6 *The* dominant variable: higher savings rates

Source: Empower Retirement LIS VI.

measure, and it's important to note that it is not driven wholly by higher incomes. That's not to say there isn't a greater tendency and ability for high-income workers to save more. But income is not the whole story.

The key driver is actually the choice architecture and the behavioral "nudges" that plan design itself creates. LIS data clearly show that workers across the income spectrum can and do achieve high levels of retirement readiness if their workplace plans adopt "full auto" plan design and escalate to savings rates of 10 percent—or more (Figure 5.6). Plan design and absolute savings rates are the prime variables determining success.

That's why most experts, myself included, advocate automatic enrollment at a minimum of 6 percent of salary, escalating steadily within two years or so to 10 percent or more. So I am pleased to see more plan sponsors moving to this higher level. This is also why the Financial Services Roundtable, one of the nation's leading advocates for retirement savings, sponsors a national campaign called "Save 10" that aims to make 10 percent or more the national norm for all workplace savings plans.

Since America's workplace savings plans average roughly a 7 percent savings rate today, moving it up to 10 percent or more may seem like a modest goal. But it's actually very ambitious. What "Save 10" calls for is a rise in workplace savings of over 40 percent, across thousands of existing workplace plans and by tens of millions of retirement savers. It is a very big deal.

Looking over the Horizon:
Toward Workplace 4.0

We can usefully think of the decade after the Pension Protection Act of 2006 as Workplace Savings 3.0, the third generation in the evolution of workplace savings in America. This period has been marked by the widespread, but not universal, adoption of the best practices to which the PPA gave solid legal sanction: automatic enrollment, automatic savings escalation, and guidance to proven default investments, all of which are plan design features more likely to take workers to full retirement readiness.

The gains scored, both in raw savings accumulated and in insights into what works, have been profound. LIS data show, for example, that more than 28 million households—those that enjoy automatic savings plans and high deferrals—are on track at the median to replace over 92 percent of their income in retirement. This is not an anomalous outlier—it's 56 million people!

Their success is proof positive of something I've said for many years: "There is nothing wrong with the 401(k) system that can't be fixed by what's right with the 401(k)." In fact, I would argue that the insights we've gained about the plan design elements that make for success may be the greatest achievements of the post-PPA decade. The challenge is to get from insight to implementation. And that's not going to be easy.

Huge gaps in our retirement system still remain. As we've seen, tens of millions of American workers have no access to savings plans on the job. And even after a decade, and despite the very powerful evidence of how auto-plan design actually works, far too many companies have yet to go full auto in their plan designs or lift their savings goals to 10 percent or more. It is as though we had discovered a vaccine against a debilitating ailment, in this case elderly poverty, but only vaccinated half our population.

Still, the PPA was a qualitative leap forward for workplace savings in America. The successful outcomes it is delivering for millions point the way toward making such successes available to all. What this vast experiment tells us is that we have essentially solved the challenge of accumulation. We now know that with full auto plan designs and deferrals over 10 percent, virtually all workers can build up enough assets to supplement Social Security and achieve reliable lifetime incomes.

The challenge now is to cover all workers and spread proven best practices across all workplace plans—not just large companies and forward-thinking small ones. That will likely require some fresh legislative and regulatory nudges for plan participants.

There is, however, positive ferment in the marketplace. America's workplace retirement system is, as always, in dynamic flux. Just as new solutions like target date funds and auto-enrollment were gestating in the early 2000s, today the industry is developing approaches for dealing with the single most glaring challenge that PPA didn't touch: the solutions and strategies to convert life savings into lifelong income.

Clearly, the main unfinished business of the second post-PPA decade will be to go beyond accumulation to find workable solutions for the far more complex, and individualized, goal of lifetime income distribution. Lifetime income solutions, in plans and beyond, strike me as the holy grail of the next generation of workplace savings in America. Done right, this could enable DC plans to match, or even surpass, the reliable incomes that traditional pensions once provided.

Fortunately, more plan sponsors and retirement providers are already experimenting with a wide variety of insured income solutions including annuities, partial annuities, deferred annuities, and non-annuity guaranteed income products beyond workplace plans and into retirement. And just as the U.S. Treasury helped spur automatic enrollment by giving it legal sanction in the late 1990s, Treasury has now given a green light for the inclusion of deferred annuities directly in workplace plans and in IRAs.

The good news, then, is that this next generation of retirement solutions—Workplace Savings 4.0—is busy being born right now in the marketplace. I believe that it should soon be helped along and ratified by regulatory and legislative action that builds on what the PPA achieved and takes workplace savings in America to a new and higher level.

The Value of Advice

Today, as individual Americans are increasingly responsible for their own financial destinies, professional investment advice is more valuable than ever before.

The trend toward defined contribution savings is roughly a generation old in the United States and rising in the United Kingdom, Canada, Australia, and other countries, shifting financial responsibility and risk from governments and employers to individuals. But, for the first time in history, DC retirement savings have also created widespread middle-class wealth. And the data make it clear that financial advice plays an irreplaceable role in helping investors shoulder this opportunity and responsibility. Industry studies suggest that investors who get advice enjoy about 1.5 percent more per year in improved performance. And through what we call the miracle of compounding, this advisor edge builds over time to deliver substantially better results.

Households that work with a financial advisor accumulate 58 percent more assets than do self-directed investors in as little as 4 to 6 years. Those working with an advisor for 7 to 14 years essentially double the wealth accumulation of do-it-yourselfers. And those drawing on advice for more than 15 years accumulate 2.7 times the wealth of those who go it alone. To make it more impressive, these are net results, after taxes and after accounting for the costs of professional advice itself.

How do advisors do it? Not by pure stock-picking. Their real value stems from the extended communication and deep collaboration with their clients that result in their clients saving twice as much—8.6 percent of income a year on average—than do unadvised investors, who set aside just 4.3 percent annually. Empower's Lifetime Income Survey found that households that don't use advice can anticipate replacing just 57 percent of their preretirement income, while those working with advisors can replace 87 percent.

Savings rates and discipline (not chasing returns, reacting emotionally to market volatility, or hunkering down in "secure" assets that yield minimal returns) are the prime variables that determine lifetime asset accumulation. Higher levels of saving, across as many years as possible, make a far more powerful difference than decisions on portfolio allocation, market timing, or choosing between active and passive strategies. These results suggest that DC workplace savings and quality financial advice fit together hand in glove.

CHAPTER 6

NEXT GENERATION DEFINED CONTRIBUTION PLANS: WORKPLACE SAVINGS 4.0, MARKET INNOVATION, AND POLICY SUPPORT

*The enterprise that does not
innovate ages and declines.*
—PETER DRUCKER

He not busy being born is busy dying.
—BOB DYLAN

Evolving steadily over more than three decades since the emergence of the first 401(k)s, America's defined contribution savings system has arguably become the greatest wages-to-wealth machine in the history of finance. Just 11 years after being blessed by the Pension Protection Act of 2006, DC savings plans have reached $7.3 trillion in assets in the first quarter of 2017, while IRAs, mainly filled by savings rolled over from DC plans, hold an additional $8.2 trillion. No other nation on earth has anything comparable.

And this tidal wave of retirement assets is still rising, even as hundreds of billions of dollars are drawn out each year to fund American retirees' current living expenses. Intense competition among providers to serve this rising wave of DC savings continues to drive positive changes for workplace savers. Fees and administrative costs of workplace savings plans, for example, have been falling for a generation (Figure 6.1). For retirement services providers, such price compression is a relentlessly rising cost of doing business, and it shows no sign of stopping.

Market-driven innovations that improve workplace plans' services and customer experience are continuous. Service providers routinely roll out easy-to-understand calculations that show how retirement savers are progressing toward their lifetime income goals. Same with better planning and analytical tools, including health cost estimators. Access to automated online investing with robo-advisors is growing. So are new offerings by workplace plans of triple-tax-free health savings accounts (HSAs) that allow those with high-deductible health plans to save money for out-of-pocket medical expenses. And more plan sponsors each year are thinking about or experimenting with ways to include annuities and other guaranteed income strategies within plans and on into workers' retirement years.

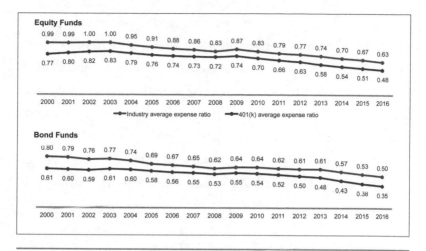

FIGURE 6.1 Price competition drives down fees for mutual funds in 401(k) plans

Source: Sean Collins, Sarah Holden, James Duvall, and Elena Barone Chism. 2016. "The Economics of Providing 401(k) Plans: Services, Fees, and Expenses, 2016." ICI Research Perspective vol 23, no. 4 (June 2017).

Bringing DB Features to DC Plans

Market forces seem, in fact, to be bringing to defined contribution plans many of the best aspects of traditional defined benefit pensions. In many plans today, for example, auto-enrollment and automatic savings escalation are getting close to matching the near-universality of the best DB plans of the past. Extensive experience now shows that very few workers deliberately choose to opt out if they are auto-enrolled in savings plans and have their savings set to rise over time. Contrary to the fears of some policy makers and plan sponsors, workers don't resent these features; they welcome them. Why? Because these nudges built into plan designs make it easier for workers to reach the goals they want to reach.

Similarly, the rapid spread of target date funds as the default choices within plans is providing millions of workplace savers access to professionally managed asset allocation. Since target date funds automatically reduce risk as their owners' retirement date nears, they require no more attention from these savers than they might have paid to the investment choices made by traditional DB pension managers. Their lifelong strategic investment patterns are built in and roll along automatically.

The Proven Path to Retirement Security

A decade after the PPA, a consensus view is emerging in the world of retirement policy. It holds that, taken together, the best practices found in fully automatic, high-savings-rate plans can achieve these plans' key goal: accumulating sufficient assets to provide a worker with reliable income replacement for life. The basic design debate is over. The results of what amounts to a vast, real-time experiment are in. Full auto plans that lift savings rates to 10 percent or more clearly can, in fact, solve the accumulation challenge. The code has been cracked.

But even though we've identified and test-driven practical, proven accumulation solutions that are working well for millions, we have a long way to go to fully implement these solutions among all workplace plans. Ten years on from the PPA's endorsement, adoption of fully automatic plan designs has slowed to a crawl. Fully 66.7 percent of large plans (5,000 or more participants) have adopted auto-enrollment for their employees' savings plans. But among employers overall, just 57.5

percent of those who offer workplace savings plans now automatically enroll their workers, and too many of these employers limit auto-enrollment in savings plans to new hires (49.6 percent). Even among large plans, barely 22 percent include automatic savings escalation in their plan designs. And auto-escalation features drop away rapidly among the savings plans offered by smaller firms (12 percent).

This failure to adopt proven plan designs has many causes: force of habit, inertia, caution, or fear of change. Many human resources and benefits executives, for example, may hesitate to propose a full auto plan design because shifting to such a model would increase their company's cost of offering matching funds once the full auto design lifts employees to saving at a much higher rate. Some CEOs might hesitate for similar reasons.

These concerns are sorely misplaced. The real risk, long-term, lies in *not* adopting proven plan designs that will bring employees reliably toward retirement readiness. Business leaders, especially CEOs, should recognize that designing workplace savings plans that have a real shot at bringing employees up to full retirement readiness is too important a decision to be delegated to HR departments or benefits planners who may feel pressure—or even compensation incentives—to contain costs. These professionals need CEO support to see and do the right thing. And even if there are added costs for increased savings matches, CEOs can feather those costs smoothly into multiyear compensation planning more easily than their HR teams might be able to do without top-level support.

Clearly, it's in the common economic interest of all businesses, large or small, and of their workers, to see near-universal adoption of fully automatic savings plan design. We would all benefit from an increased sense of security, more widespread ownership, stable consumption in retirement, and more rapid economic growth funded by higher savings. But as we see the uptake of fully automatic plan designs slowing down, further progress will require fresh rounds of market innovation, regulatory guidance, and legislative support.

At Empower Retirement, we've laid out a broad set of goals for the next generation of workplace savings—Workplace 4.0—building, as earlier generations did, on great ideas already proven in the market or emerging from market innovation. We are pushing for reforms that can finish the job the PPA did so much to advance. We aim to first imagine, and then help flesh out, a robust workplace savings system that reaches all working Americans. We're advocating for reform and innovations that go beyond accumulation to solve the even more complex challenge of distribution, reliable lifetime income, the holy grail of twenty-first-century workplace savings. Figure 6.2 shows that vision in a nutshell.

First, Do No Harm

Future tax reforms must preserve and expand the existing savings incentives that have helped fuel the rise of today's multitrillion-dollar workplace savings system. Given the undeniable need to increase, not discourage, more retirement savings, the tax deferrals that help people fill up their 401(k)s or IRAs should be sacrosanct—politically untouchable. And the truth is, these incentives actually do foster family and personal solvency, which, in turn, strengthen the nation's whole balance sheet.

- Preserve and expand all existing savings incentives and correct the false "scoring" and 10-year "window" used today to account for the cost of savings deferrals.
- Close the "access gap" and provide workplace savings to all—by supporting legislation to facilitate multiple employer plans, "Starter" 401(k)s, and auto-IRAs at the national level.
- Provide larger—and refundable—Saver's Credits, additional tax credits to employers who establish plans, and credits to part-time, freelance, and contract workers who establish IRAs.
- Require the adoption of "full auto" plan design as the norm—system-wide—while also strengthening legal safe harbors for plan sponsors. Establish an industry norm of 10%+ deferral.
- Support greater adoption of lifetime income options—in plans and beyond—backed up by tax preferences for workers who choose guaranteed income.
- Allow retirees to make tax-free withdrawals from qualified plans if they are used to cover health insurance or medical care.

FIGURE 6.2 Workplace Savings 4.0: Reforms to keep America's retirement promise

We should never pit national solvency and personal solvency against each other, as some recent tax reform proposals have done. It is terribly shortsighted policy to suggest cuts to personal savings incentives to "pay for" other, unrelated tax breaks. To reduce that constant temptation, we also need to correct the misleading and potentially damaging ways that Congress currently accounts for savings incentives in its budgeting process. The following box, "Honest Arithmetic for Savings Tax Deferrals," gives a brief look at why that arcane "inside baseball" element of congressional budgeting matters a great deal.

Honest Arithmetic for Savings Tax Deferrals

Just when we can begin to see the outlines of a much more successful twenty-first-century retirement system, we face continued risks from the wrongheaded methods that Congress uses to account for, or "score," the cost of retirement tax incentives to the U.S. Treasury.

For decades, dating back to the Budget Act of 1974, Congress has essentially treated the tax "deferrals" enjoyed by savers in workplace plans or IRAs as if they were identical to such true tax "expenditures" as the tax rebates that people claim and receive for mortgage interest or charitable deductions (Figure 6.3).

But unlike these "once-and-gone" tax breaks, deferrals for retirement savings only postpone taxes. They do not "forgive" them—in fact, far from it. Assets in qualified retirement savings plans or IRAs do collect capital gains and dividend income for many years, even decades, tax free. But the moment someone takes a distribution of assets, they are taxed as ordinary income. Uncle Sam's Treasury gets a very significant share of deferred taxes back over the full life cycle of this arrangement.

But by lumping savings deferrals with true tax expenditures, Congress's current budget methods grossly overestimate their cost. This makes the savings incentives that help all American workers a ripe target—a nearly irresistible "go-to" honey pot—for members of Congress looking to "pay for" other, unrelated tax reductions.

Worse, congressional budget calculations are limited to a 10-year window. This means that in calculating what

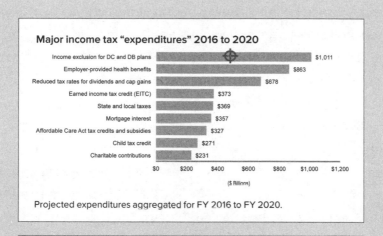

Major income tax "expenditures" 2016 to 2020

Income exclusion for DC and DB plans	$1,011
Employer-provided health benefits	$863
Reduced tax rates for dividends and cap gains	$678
Earned income tax credit (EITC)	$373
State and local taxes	$369
Mortgage interest	$357
Affordable Care Act tax credits and subsidies	$327
Child tax credit	$271
Charitable contributions	$231

$0 $200 $400 $600 $800 $1,000 $1,200

($ Billions)

Projected expenditures aggregated for FY 2016 to FY 2020.

FIGURE 6.3 Flawed budget estimates lump savings deferrals in with true tax expenditures

Source: Congressional Joint Committee on Taxation, Estimates of Federal Tax Expenditures for Fiscal Years 2016-2020, January 2017.

any policy "costs," Congress can look out just 10 years—and not one day beyond. Retirement savings, of course, accumulate for decades before being drawn down and then generating long-term tax flows back to the Treasury.

According to a study by the American Society of Pension Professionals and Actuaries (ASPPA), these budget methods may be exaggerating workplace plans' cost to the Treasury by as much as 50 percent. This makes savings tax deferrals seem to be among the most expensive expenditures in any budget Congress passes—an estimated $500 billion just from 2014 to 2017. That's a huge and very tempting target for budget-cutters.

No surprise then that the tax reform proposal put forward in 2014 would have cut incentives for retirement savings by roughly $250 billion over its first 10 years.

That bill, fortunately, proved dead on arrival. But until we correct the arcane budget methods Congress uses to account for retirement savings, the threat of new cuts will recur every time broad tax reform is proposed.

At a minimum, Congress should amend the 1974 Budget Act to draw a sharp distinction between true expenditures and deferrals. We should measure the true costs of retirement deferrals over a full life cycle—as long as 50+ years. This is not some special interest favor that Congress would be granting. The "ask" in this case is simply for honest arithmetic in a policy area that affects nearly 125 million working Americans. And this long-overdue course correction should come before the next major round of tax or pension reform so we can make policy on the basis of reality, not a broken, outdated metric.

I believe it would be totally legitimate for congressional budget estimators to go further and take account of two additional benefits that retirement savings clearly bring. One would be higher economic growth and increased tax revenues, produced by channeling workers' savings through our dynamic capital markets. (See Chapter 8, "Workplace Savings, Capital Markets, and Economic Growth.") A second major benefit these savings produce, but which current budgeting methods fail to account for, is lower future costs to the Treasury from retirees seeking means-tested public aid like Medicaid.

In a very real and quantifiable sense, every penny of savings spurred by tax deferrals is one less penny that savers will ever claim from the Treasury, until they have drained their savings to the bone. So before we do any

> major tax or pension reform, let's take these very real
> benefits into account; call it "reality-based budgeting." We
> owe it to ourselves to get this right.

Apart from protecting existing savings incentives, the most pressing goal for future retirement policy should be to close the yawning "coverage gap" and provide access to some form of payroll deduction savings plan for the tens of millions of working Americans who have no on-the-job savings plans today. We can do that by adopting legislation to require that all employers provide automatic IRA payroll savings deductions on the job. We can pass legislation enabling unrelated small businesses to band together to form multiple-employer savings plans. We should be open to fresh ideas to meet this challenge—at the national level.

Unless Congress does act to close the workplace savings coverage gap at the national level, we can anticipate continued movement by some states to try government-sponsored plans aimed at covering the uncovered. This could lead to a complex, far less effective patchwork of state solutions, exempt from the investor protections already provided under ERISA.

We could easily see the emergence of an unfair, two-tier retirement savings structure. Workers in large firms would enjoy robust ERISA-regulated 401(k)s with high returns, while millions of small business employees would be relegated to second-rate state-sponsored plans with lower returns, higher costs, and the risk of never reaching retirement readiness.

For all these reasons, we believe that Congress should take the rise of these new state plans as a wake-up call to provide national solutions, including creative ways to offer the large, fast-growing number of part-time, contract, and "gig economy" workers options for direct deduction to retirement savings from their 1099 payments. Ideally, I would like to see every worker who is subject to pay FICA taxes to Social Security also enjoy the option of saving for retirement easily and automatically.

A third step toward the vision for Workplace 4.0 would be to use regulatory and legislative support to require all existing workplace savings plans to adopt fully automatic plan design features. This could be achieved through a combination of regulatory guidance and leadership, plus a new round of pension reform from Congress. The logic of requiring these best practices by law seems to me as irrefutable as the mandate we impose on families to vaccinate their children against polio, measles, and other serious diseases. Once you know what works, there's almost a fiduciary duty to advocate for its universal adoption.

Ten years after the PPA, the time has come for major new pension legislation that can apply proven best practices to all workplace plans, and increase the tax-based incentives for employers to offer plans and for participants to enroll and save more. Increasing incentives to employers for offering plans and for matching workers' savings makes sense precisely because the companies that do these things are directly contributing to the larger national goal of retirement security for all.

The next major pension reform should not only finish the work the PPA did in solving the challenge of accumulation, it should go on to offer support for greater adoption of lifetime income options, in plans and beyond. And it should offer strong tax advantages for workers who choose to purchase guaranteed income product options that draw down a retirement portfolio. We might, for example, allow retirees to draw the first $10,000 in income from such guaranteed sources tax free, so as to powerfully encourage them to consider buying such income products.

What Could Workplace 4.0 Policy Reforms Achieve?

To assess the potential impact of the reforms proposed by Empower Retirement's Workplace Savings 4.0 policy agenda, we asked Jack VanDerhei of the Employee Benefit Research Institute (EBRI) to run them through EBRI's highly respected Retirement Security Projection Model®, a tool that analyzes retirement income adequacy under various policy scenarios. The findings were powerful.

EBRI's model suggests that a full Workplace Savings 4.0 reform agenda could lift annual retirement savings in America by nearly $700 billion dollars a year within three years—with continuing gains in later years (Figure 6.4). That is a huge increase—133 percent in fact—in the savings flowing through qualified retirement plans and IRAs into our stock and bond markets; it would be a major spur to new capital formation coming entirely from retirement savers.

The added savings from these reforms could raise total American retirement savings by more than $5 trillion by the middle of the 2020s, providing a steadily rising flow of investment capital to our securities markets. As we'll see in Chapter 8, these added savings, in turn, would contribute to funding higher investment, rising productivity, and economic growth,

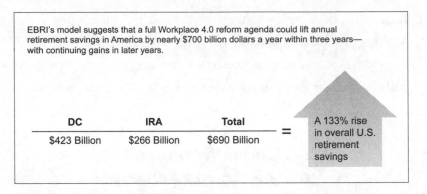

FIGURE 6.4   Impact of Workplace Savings 4.0 policies on retirement

Source: EBRI estimates.

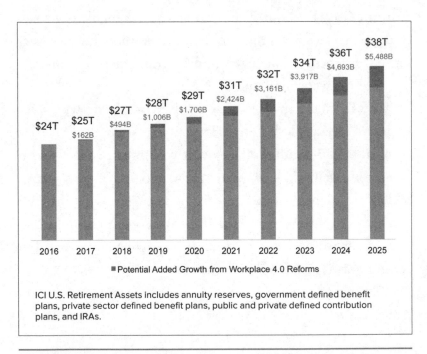

FIGURE 6.5   Total U.S. retirement assets with projected growth from Workplace Savings 4.0 reforms

Source: EBRI estimates.

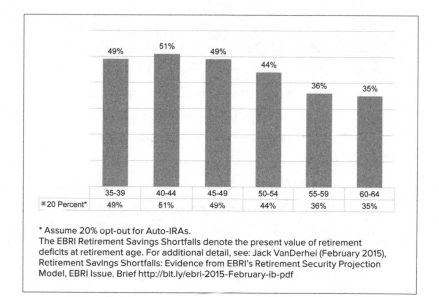

	35-39	40-44	45-49	50-54	55-59	60-64
■ 20 Percent*	49%	51%	49%	44%	36%	35%

* Assume 20% opt-out for Auto-IRAs.
The EBRI Retirement Savings Shortfalls denote the present value of retirement deficits at retirement age. For additional detail, see: Jack VanDerhei (February 2015), Retirement Savings Shortfalls: Evidence from EBRI's Retirement Security Projection Model, EBRI Issue. Brief http://bit.ly/ebri-2015-February-ib-pdf

FIGURE 6.6 How much Workplace Savings 4.0 reforms would reduce retirement savings shortfalls— by age group

Source: EBRI Retirement Security Protection Model® Version 2659.

while providing retirees with more robust assets from which to draw lifelong income (Figure 6.5).

From the point of view of working Americans, EBRI's analysis suggests that the 4.0 reforms would take a huge bite out of the nation's retirement savings shortfall, reducing it by nearly 50 percent for all workers 30 to 50 years old, and by more than 30 percent even for older workers 55 to 64 years old. Younger workers, of course, have many more years for contributions to grow before they need to draw on them for retirement income. But Workplace Savings 4.0 reforms would offer significant help even for those within just a few years of retirement (Figure 6.6).

Perhaps the single most powerful impact suggested in the Workplace Savings 4.0 agenda is that of allowing retirees to draw funds from their qualified plans tax free if used for medical insurance or other health costs. That such a change would have great weight is not wholly surprising, since many estimates of total healthcare costs for retirees range from $250,000 on up.

Taken together, Workplace Savings 4.0 reforms would effectively solve most of the challenge of inadequate retirement income, except for those retirees stricken with chronic illness. According to EBRI's analysis, a majority of the savings shortfall that would remain, even if 4.0 reforms were adopted, is due to the crushing costs of long-term nursing home care. This is a highly unpredictable cost/risk for most people and is currently very difficult to insure against. Fostering the growth of an efficient, nationwide market for affordable long-term-care insurance is a worthy goal that will likely require major federal legislation so retirement savers can better protect their futures.

Adoption of the full 4.0 agenda would not be a perfect solution. It would leave long-term care as the last frontier of full retirement security. But it would be a huge step forward, and it would provide confidence-building proof that Americans can take on major challenges—and solve them.

Lifetime Income: The Holy Grail

The core goal of what we call Workplace Savings 4.0—the "holy grail" of the next generation of workplace savings in America—is to convert accumulated *assets* into guaranteed lifetime *income*. Through the same mix of market-driven innovation, academic research, and smart policy formation that led to the PPA, we can achieve in DC plans the lifetime income predictability that a minority of workers once enjoyed through traditional pensions.

Unfortunately, there is no one-size-fits-all model for attaining guaranteed lifetime income. Nor should there be in a dynamic and diverse financial services marketplace. What we will see, I hope, is a cross-silo collaboration of asset managers, insurers, and financial advisors that delivers a broad range of guaranteed-income solutions. We can foresee lively competition that will apply effective and transparent algorithms to convert tens of trillions of dollars in retirement assets into secure individual income streams or "personal pensions," customized to fit a wide variety of individual and family goals.

Guaranteed lifetime income is at the core of Workplace Savings 4.0 because it is the basic goal of all retirement savings programs and the deepest concern of American workers themselves. Survey after survey tells us that most Americans' greatest fear about retirement is running out of money before they run out of time. In fact, multiple surveys tell us that people fear poverty or severe financial stress in old age more than they fear death itself.

And the challenge of drawing down a lifetime's savings so that it lasts a lifetime is far more daunting, and individualized, than that of piling up assets while still working. Post-PPA experience suggests that we essentially know what it takes to accumulate enough raw savings: full auto plans with 10-percent-plus savings rates will do that. But the PPA provided virtually no guidance, guidelines, or policy support for how to convert those assets into reliable lifetime income, leaving it to individuals to figure it out.

It is particularly important that we focus on converting defined contribution savings into income today, because for a generation, we have experienced the steady erosion of traditional guaranteed income sources.

As of 2016, current retirees draw nearly two-thirds of their retirement income from Social Security and defined benefit pensions. But both of these sources will continue to shrink in terms of income replacement for decades into the future. Defined benefit pensions are steadily disappearing except for government workers, and even in the public sector, they face dim prospects. With multiple funding crises afflicting public DB plans—in Puerto Rico, Detroit, Illinois, and many other cities and states—there is a rising drumbeat for these programs to be reformed or even converted into DC plans.

What's more, the contribution of Social Security to income replacement is projected under current law to fall from roughly 36 percent today to just over 29 percent in 2037 because of increases in the age of eligibility and deductions for the rising cost of Medicare benefits. That's not to mention the longer-term challenge of Social Security system solvency (see Chapter 2: "Retirement's Bedrock: Social Security"), which will require congressional action for current benefit schedules to be honored.

The diminishing ability of DB pensions and Social Security to replace future retirees' incomes is opening a guaranteed income gap that will continue to expand in coming years. For most Americans today, and for nearly all private-sector workers in the future, DC plans will be the primary source of retirement income. That's why it's critical that we get to work on ways to dramatically improve the ability of DC plans to step into this widening gap and deliver reliable lifetime income solutions for generations to come.

Fortunately, the policy, academic, and professional practice communities are already engaged in debate and experimentation to address the challenges of distribution and lifetime income. Broad agreement is emerging that we must expand the range of retirement income solutions in plans to include a full range of fixed, variable, and deferred-income annuities along with guaranteed payout plans that can be customized by investors and their financial advisors.

By dramatically increasing the availability of guaranteed lifetime income options in defined contribution plans, we could replicate one of the best elements of traditional defined benefit pensions—assured flows of lifetime income.

Indeed, the most significant advantage of DB plans may be that by linking all participants in a common pool to purchase lifetime income, these plans can accurately estimate the collective lifespan of participants, as a group, and match investments and assets to that average lifespan. By contrast, individual 401(k) savers can't be sure how long they will live. Workers in retirement must then either save more or draw down income very cautiously from their savings because of longevity risk, the very real possibility that they may live far longer than their peers and so outlive their savings.

Incorporating pooled lifetime income options like annuities into DC plans could dramatically reduce every saver's individual longevity risk. What's more, working income guarantees into a DC plan would also limit another key hazard that all retirees face—"sequence of returns" risk. That is the damage that a series of sharply down years in the securities markets can inflict if they come early in retirement.

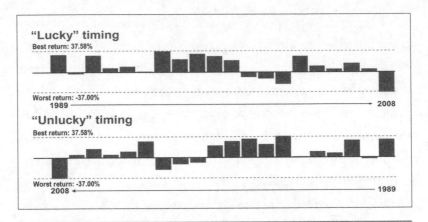

FIGURE 6.7 Sequence-of-returns risk: the retirement timing "lottery"

Source: Putnam Investments estimates.

Managing "Sequence of Returns" Risk

The most dangerous, and too-little-known, risk to retirement savers lies in the sequence of investment returns in markets in the years just after retirement. Figure 6.7 shows two series of investment returns. The top shows the historical returns of the S&P 500 from 1989 to 2008. The bottom sequence shows those same annual returns in reverse order. Both series have the same *average* return of 10.36 percent over 20 years. But the impact of these returns on a retirement portfolio is radically different.

To illustrate the impact that a returns sequence can make, we show a hypothetical all-equity portfolio worth $1 million invested from 1989 to 2008 in the S&P 500, and then reverse the sequence of returns. If the investor retires in 1989, his timing is wonderfully lucky. Starting with a portfolio of $1 million, withdrawing 5 percent a year, and stepping up at 3 percent

"Lucky" timing		
	$1,343,519	Total income
	10.36%	Average return
	$3,074,205	Ending value
"Unlucky" timing		
	$1,196,731	Total income
	10.36%	Average return
	$0	Ending value

FIGURE 6.8 The impact of sequence-of-returns risk

Source: Putnam Investments estimates.

annually to cover inflation, his investments return more than $1.3 million in income over 20 years, taking advantage of strongly positive early-year returns to total more than $3 million at the end of 20 years (Figure 6.8).

When we flip this sequence of these returns so it runs from 2008 to 1989, the average yearly return over the period is exactly the same: 10.36 percent. But if we assume the same initial withdrawals and inflation adjustments, this unlucky (and ill-timed) retiree would be flat broke after just 19 years after drawing just $1.1 million in income from the original $1 million portfolio.

That's sequence-of-returns risk in a stark example. It's the chronological equivalent of a lottery ticket. So how can we manage this risk? There are many ways, but for simplicity's sake let's just consider what a retiree might achieve by partially annuitizing his retirement assets.

In this case, the investor converts 50 percent of his initial $1 million portfolio into a guaranteed income product and draws the remainder of his income from the remaining equity

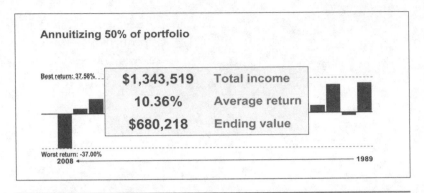

Annuitizing 50% of portfolio

Best return: 37.58%

$1,343,519   Total income

10.36%   Average return

$680,218   Ending value

Worst return: -37.00%
2008 ←   → 1989

FIGURE 6.9   Insuring against sequence-of-returns risk:
the unlucky (but secure) investor

Source: Putnam Investments estimates.

portfolio (Figure 6.9). Let's further assume that he has to endure
the "unlucky" sequence of returns we've seen above.

Here's the result: The total 20-year income matches that
of the investor who has a lucky sequence of returns—over $1.3
million—and the initial $500,000 in equity assets actually
grows to over $680,000.

How is that possible? The reason is that committing 50
percent of his assets to guaranteed income helps avoid half of
the huge initial losses in this sequence. And since substantial
income is drawn from the guaranteed source, the equity portfolio is drawn down more slowly, leaving the bulk of those assets
more time to recover from the initial difficult years.

Admittedly, there's a much smaller equity balance at the
end than the lucky investor would achieve. But bear this in
mind: This unlucky investor has survived a dangerous sequence
of returns; his liquid assets have risen, not fallen, let alone been
totally drained, and he still owns a guaranteed income contract
that provides a substantial degree of lifetime income security.

There are, of course, fees and expenses associated with any guaranteed income product. And such products are subject to the claims-paying ability of the insurance issuer. But as this example demonstrates, guaranteed income options in a retirement plan can mitigate the risk posed by a damaging sequence of returns while also fending off the worst retirement risk of all: total depletion of assets in late old age. Such significant personal and social gains seem to me to merit serious policy and tax incentive supports.

Solving the "Annuity Puzzle"

Despite the powerful benefits that adding some form of guaranteed income can provide, retirement savers have not exactly rushed to buy annuities. Nor have most plan sponsors chosen to offer any form of income guarantees in their plans, though the most recent Lifetime Income Solutions Survey by Willis Towers Watson did show that over half of plan sponsors anticipate offering a guaranteed income solution in the future. In the meantime:

- One-third provide in-plan managed account services with a non-guaranteed payout.
- Only 22 percent offer an in-plan asset allocation option with a guaranteed minimum withdrawal or annuity component.
- Only 6 percent of employers offer out-of-plan annuities at the time of retirement.
- Less than 10 percent offer an in-plan deferred annuity investment option.

Why haven't workers and plan sponsors more fully embraced annuities or other forms of guaranteed income solutions? Given the powerful advantages of pooling longevity risk, that's something of a mystery, which is why economists call the reluctance of consumers to buy guaranteed income products "the annuity puzzle."

Two powerful reasons that plan sponsors cite are fiduciary risk (81 percent) and cost (67 percent), precisely the impediments that once held back the adoption of automatic enrollment and savings escalation in the years before the PPA. For individual investors, guaranteed income solutions have too often been associated with complexity, opacity, high distribution costs, and hidden fees. Given the choice, even most defined benefit plan participants choose lump-sum payouts over annuitization.

Consumers are often reluctant to sacrifice liquidity or to let go of the wealth illusion that large lump sums of money can generate, especially compared with the modest returns that annuities offer in today's ultra-low interest-rate environment. Some also fear the single-provider risk that an insurance company could fail to meet its annuity obligations. Those fears need to be addressed.

The challenge for America's next major pension reform, then, is to go beyond ensuring that all American workers have access to fully automatic savings plans on their jobs. Workplace Savings 4.0 should offer a framework of guidelines, guardrails, and incentives that extend beyond workers' careers to help them successfully convert their life savings into lifetime income.

CHAPTER 7

AMERICA'S RETIREMENT SYSTEM IN A GLOBAL CONTEXT

*It says something about this new global economy
that* USA Today *now reports every morning
on the day's events in Asian markets.*
—**LARRY SUMMERS**

In the leading global league tables of national retirement systems (Figure 7.1), Uncle Sam doesn't seem to have much to brag about (We're number 13!), or so these pension experts would have us believe.

So let's widen our lens and take a brief look at how the retirement savings system we've built in this country actually ranks in a global context. Despite our shortfalls, as we will see, we're very much on the right track.

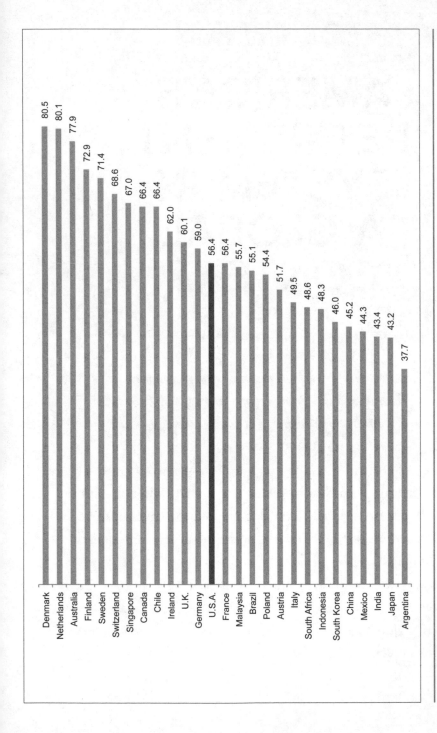

FIGURE 7.1 2016 Global Pension Index: How did each country fare?

Source: Melbourne Mercer Global Pension Index, 2016.

Global retirement finance surveys typically rank the United States in the middle of major nations' retirement systems, with their focus mainly on the 25 largest nations and economies. The retirement savings systems of the next 150+ countries are simply too small to merit serious attention.

But even though these analyses judge the U.S. retirement system to be at the midrange of their *qualitative* rankings, due to our well-known coverage shortfalls and unequal income replacement ratios, the United States takes top billing in any *quantitative* ranking because of the staggering, multitrillion-dollar scale of the funded assets that back both our traditional DB pensions and our DC workplace savings plans.

For example, actuarial consultants Willis Towers Watson inform us that the world's top 22 retirement finance markets comprise some $36 trillion in funded pension assets. But while the United States accounts for a bit less than 40 percent of those nations' combined economic output, we have accumulated fully 62 percent of the developed world's retirement assets.

These numbers alone suggest that we take the litany we hear from media and academic naysayers with a grain of salt. Too often, the message is that the United States is uniquely vulnerable to an imminent retirement "crisis" while better-prepared economies around the world are somehow immune. As we'll see, a closer look at the data suggests quite the opposite.

America's public and private retirement systems do have imperfections, some of them quite serious, but all of them are eminently correctable if we simply spread the best practices in these existing plans system-wide. So if we want to decode the true significance of global pension rankings, we need to unpack their underlying data and their assumptions about the future and draw our own conclusions.

In this chapter, we'll talk about pension architecture (defined benefit vs. defined contribution structures), about real funding versus political promises, about national styles of asset allocation (stocks, bonds, alternatives), and about actuarial sustainability. What we'll find is that far from being the "sick man" of global retirement finance, the United States, on a relative basis, and over the long term, is one of the best-prepared nations on earth.

The most striking feature of global retirement system rankings is that many of the best-regarded systems are found in a handful of small, wealthy countries in Northern Europe—the Netherlands, Sweden, Denmark, Switzerland, Norway, and Iceland. These are some of the most prosperous economies on earth, as measured by per capita income, economic stability, and income equality. It stands to reason that they should have well-organized retirement systems, and they surely deserve high marks for their far-sighted preparation for retirement.

The United States can certainly learn from their experience and adapt some of their best ideas. But it's totally unrealistic politically to think this country would ever import whole-cloth the retirement models of these small, ethnically homogenous nations to a continent-straddling colossus with a multi-ethnic population of 330 million people, high legal immigration, vastly varying regional economies, and a GDP of $20 trillion. By contrast:

- Sweden's entire population would fit into Los Angeles County; its GDP is smaller than that of Massachusetts.

- Norway has socked away roughly $1 trillion in an oil-fueled pension fund for its 5 million citizens; its GDP is slightly smaller than that of North Carolina.
- Iceland's population of 332,000 is the same size as metropolitan Lincoln, Nebraska; its GDP is less than that of Vermont.

There are some substantial economies to be found on these pension rankings—for example, the United Kingdom, Australia, Canada, France, Germany, and Japan, with their widely varying ways of saving for and financing retirement. There are also some surprising no-shows on these lists, including Brazil, Russia, India, and China—the BRIC countries that were until recently touted as the key drivers of global growth in the twenty-first century. To date, though, these nations simply haven't developed substantial retirement savings systems.

We can see very clearly that pay-as-you-go pension systems all over the world face rising pressure from the relentless forces of global aging. Rising life spans are lifting the number of retiree recipients, while the number of active young workers paying taxes stalls or even shrinks. The "support ratios" in many nations are becoming steadily heavier every year. This will inevitably force either massive tax hikes (among already highly taxed nations such as France or Italy) or the kind of deep benefit cuts that aggravate social tension and may foment political crises.

As Figure 7.2 illustrates, nations like France, Germany, the United Kingdom, and Japan, whose systems rely mainly on tax flows from current workers, not on investments, face pension liabilities two to three times larger than their total national output. Meeting these liabilities poses a huge challenge. And there's ample reason to expect that many of these nations' seemingly

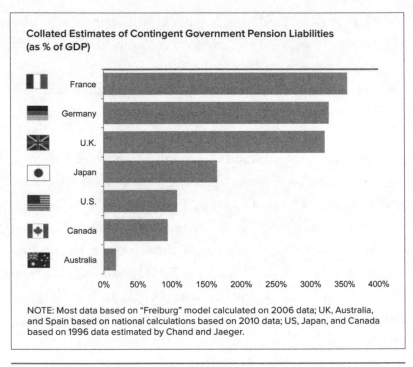

FIGURE 7.2 Some governments face huge liabilities

Source: Kaier and Muller (Freiburg University), DNB, OECD, Citi Research from Global Perspectives & Solutions, March 2016.

generous public pay-as-you-go pension programs will have to be cut back substantially. In very sharp contrast, Australia's mandatory national retirement savings system leaves that country with the lowest future retirement liability-to-GDP ratio among major nations.

With retirement liabilities roughly equal to our annual GDP, the United States does face serious challenges from rising longevity and an aging population; the need for action to make Social Security solvent is the most salient example. But America's retirement liabilities are far lighter as a share of our economy than those facing most of our major trading partners and rivals. What's more, America enjoys another advantage almost unique in the developed world. We have a relatively younger and still-growing population. Much of the rest of the developed world faces a "baby bust," and some countries face absolute population decline, even implosion, over the course of the twenty-first century.

Retirement Finance Architecture

The compilers of these global retirement tables are generally agnostic on the questions of whether pension systems are funded by real investment assets or depend on pay-as-you-go tax transfers. They also don't distinguish between DB and DC models.

What's critical is whether DB plans are fully or only partially funded. But there is a major difference between pay-as-you-go systems based wholly on taxes from current workers and prefunded retirement systems (DB, DC, or hybrid) that draw their future income from real savings invested in stocks, bonds, and other financial assets.

Taken at face value, it may seem that many national pension systems, like public sector DB pensions for state and city workers in the United States, offer both broad coverage and generous income replacement ratios. But too many of these promised benefits are not backed up by any tangible assets. They are pay-as-you-go systems dependent on future taxes, or, in the private sector, future earnings. Pay-as-you-go systems are not pension *funds*, they are pension *promises* that politicians and future generations of workers are on the hook to keep, or not.

This variety of global pension systems is healthy in the sense that having these varied policy approaches provides an ongoing global laboratory that's currently testing which plan design and funding practices work best. We can, and should, draw lessons from the lived experience of other nations, their retirees, and their system designs so we can adopt their best features—and avoid their pitfalls.

America's Demographic Advantage

As we move to and through the 2020s, America's demographic advantage over global competitors will become much more pronounced than it is today. Simply put, the United States enjoys vastly more promising long-term demographic trends than most of our major trading partners (Figure 7.3).

America not only enjoys a higher birth rate than Europe, Japan, Russia, and China, the country allows more legal immigration—well over 1 million a year—than the rest of the developed world combined. As a result, America in 2020 will have a still-growing working-age population and will be heading toward a total population well over 400 million people by mid-century.

By contrast, the populations of China, Japan, Russia, and much of Europe will be in decline by 2020. China will almost surely become old before it becomes rich—with an internal "nation" of nearly 340 million people over age 65 by mid-century and a per capita GDP still likely to be less than one-third of America's. Japan, China, Italy, Germany, and some other advanced nations may well experience a dramatic population collapse by century's end—but not the United States.

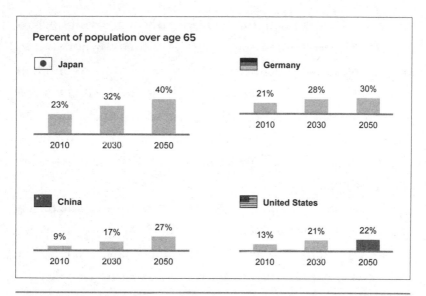

FIGURE 7.3   As key trading partners age, America will remain (relatively) young well into the twenty-first century

Source: U.S. Census Bureau, International Database, 2010.

Demographers tell us that by 2050, roughly one in three citizens of developed nations in Asia and Europe will be over 65 but only one in five Americans will be. All through the twenty-first century, in other words, America will be relatively younger than our major global rivals. We will be better able to sustain both a robust Social Security system and a strong, near-universal system of private retirement savings.

Retirement System Change Is Glacially Slow

As with any longstanding economic architecture, most nations' retirement systems change slowly; inertia is as powerful a force in national system design as it is in individual savings behavior. So while the United States long ago shifted a majority of its retirement assets to defined contribution plans, pension plans in Canada, Japan, and the Netherlands are still over 94 percent DB. Even in the United Kingdom, where DB pension shortfalls are substantial and a government-supported migration toward DC is well underway, fully 82 percent of retirement assets are still in DB plans.

Only a handful of countries have so far shifted the majority of their retirement assets to the defined contribution model, notably Australia (87 percent) and some smaller nations like New Zealand and Switzerland, which has a unique collective DC/DB hybrid system. A few emerging market countries like Chile, South Africa, and Singapore are also moving to adopt mainly DC structures. And Australia is particularly noteworthy because it has achieved near-universal pension coverage through a mandatory defined contribution savings system called "superannuation" that looks very much like our Workplace Savings 4.0 reform proposals.

One often-cited flaw in current DC systems is that many workers now entering retirement have failed for a variety of reasons to accumulate enough money to replace their preretirement incomes for life. Some entered into DC savings systems at midcareer and had only 15 or 20 years for their assets to build up. Others saved at too low a rate or saw their investment balances eroded by high fees. Some also made damaging investment choices that were either too bold or too cautious. Some withdrew funds prematurely or opted out of savings plans altogether.

Another fair critique of global DC systems may be that the transition to a defined contribution structure was financed through substantial cuts to traditional pay-as-you-go state pension systems. That, however, is not what happened in the United States.

The American migration from DB to DC was evolutionary, with competitive market forces and service innovation driving down costs without drawing a dime away from the fairly robust traditional pensions that Social Security provides for lower-income workers. With no explicit planning, the United States evolved a fairly well-balanced public/private retirement finance architecture that drew on both human and financial capital—the "twin-engine" hybrid we discussed in Chapter 2.

Asset Allocations Vary Widely Among Nations

Retirement systems are also heavily influenced by the financial structures of the nations that sponsor them. For example, in East Asia and Continental Europe stock and bond markets are not nearly as deep, widely owned, liquid, or reliable as those in the United States. All but the largest, most global companies in these countries rely mainly on the banking system, not on capital markets, for financing. So if most private companies in a country sell relatively little equity, and issue few fixed-income securities, what can their pension funds invest in?

By parsing the data, we see that retirement savings in these bank-dominated financial markets are largely allocated to debt securities issued by governments and, to a lesser degree, banks and insurance companies. But many governments, banks, and insurers in these nations face long-term challenges to their own solvency and creditworthiness.

In the wake of the global financial crisis, governments have issued record volumes of debt. Meanwhile, most banks in Europe and Asia have not been substantially recapitalized, and insurers in these regions are likewise under stress, notably from near-zero or negative interest rates. Well-grounded concern about the sustainability of these debts is straining sovereign debt credit ratings, driving currency valuations, and stoking fears about whether these national retirement systems can keep their pension promises to their people without huge tax hikes or benefit cuts.

Traditionally, pension funds typically have "laddered" fixed-income securities to match their liabilities with the income streams produced by these bonds. DB systems in the Netherlands and in Japan, for example, allocate 54 percent and 59 percent of their assets respectively mainly to bank and government bonds. DC systems in the United States and Australia, by contrast, have limited their fixed-income exposure to 22 percent and 14 percent respectively.

Today, of course, we're living through very abnormal, even unprecedented times.

On top of the pressures of demographics, public and private sector retirement funds now need to consider growing interest-rate risks. With interest rates at record lows, pension managers who traditionally relied on "safe" fixed-income investments are taking increasing risk themselves to generate sufficient income to meet their funds' liabilities.

Pension funds have long preferred to invest in bonds over stocks, because they were perceived as a safe asset class. And government debt has long been seen as the safest investment of all. But with over $13 trillion in fixed-income instruments worldwide actually delivering negative yield (as of late 2016), these once-safe investments can actually erode pension funds' principal.

And government debt is famously subject to political risk. For example, the sharp uptick in interest rates that followed the election of Donald Trump in November 2016 cut more than $1 trillion from the value of the global bond markets within days—some "safety"! No wonder those responsible for securing future retirement income streams are looking for alternatives and taking greater risk.

With interest rates at multidecade lows, and public and private debt soaring, pension plans around the world have, through their massive purchases of government debt, exposed themselves to historically unprecedented risk concentration. Many nations have small, less-liquid stock markets that limit their ability to invest in equities. So pension managers in these nations have now responded by going further out on the risk spectrum. Over the past two decades, many pension managers around the world have cut back on both stock and bond allocations in favor of higher-yielding but potentially more volatile alternatives such as real estate assets, private equity, and other nontraditional investments.

Twenty years ago, pension funds globally were 90 percent allocated to stocks and bonds, with allocations to alternative investments limited to the high single digits. Today, alternatives account for nearly a quarter of global pension fund assets, and this allocation is rising as plan sponsors, struggling with low interest rates, reach for yield in an attempt to keep their pension promises.

Sustainability, Anyone?

At the end of the day, the ultimate determinant of success for any retirement finance system is its economic sustainability—its long-term ability to deliver reliable lifelong income for retirees.

But retirement finance surveys are generally a snapshot of the here and now, not of a system's long-term viability. This may be why the United States tends to end up in the middle ranks in many surveys. America gets dinged because of the high number of workers who lack any workplace savings options and because our replacement ratios vary widely among workers who do have plans. What's more, our system is a patchwork of Social Security and DB and DC plans for both public and private sector workers.

The American retirement finance system is improvised, iterative, and evolutionary. But far from being a liability, this diverse mix may prove to be its greatest asset because such a large share of Americans' future income will be drawn from investments in productive private businesses.

Our defined contribution system is based on individual ownership of financial assets. The asset allocation of participants in these plans does need to be guided over a working lifetime from high-risk/high-return equities to lower-risk/lower-return fixed-income investments. Participants should be guided along a glide path that extends from their first job up to and beyond their retirement date.

We all know that investing in capital markets inevitably entails risk. Yet over multidecade time frames, that risk can be carefully calibrated and reduced as workers draw closer to retirement and need to convert life savings into reliable lifetime income. This is what the workplace savings industry exists to do.

With governments around the world (ours included) strapped for cash and taking on massive debt in the wake of the global financial crisis, many observers view their unfunded, or underfunded, pension liabilities as a growing source of systemic risk, not only for retirement finance systems, but for national economies and governments' own solvency. The American system, by contrast, rests on a strong foundation of real investments in private industry.

Where Are the Funded Pension Assets? In the United States

While the United States may rank down the list of retirement finance benefits, it ranks at the very top for sustainability. According to Willis Towers Watson, the world's top 22 retirement finance markets comprise some $36 trillion, with aggregate pension assets of 62 percent of GDP. The United States, with 121 percent of GDP, ranks right at the top (Table 7.1).

With funded pension assets (DB and DC) at levels 8 to 10 times higher than the next largest national pension pool, and a top-two ranking for pension savings measured as a percentage of GDP, the United States is a retirement finance giant.

By comparison, massive and wealthy economies such as Germany and France seem woefully unprepared. Workers in these countries have traditionally looked to insurance products such as annuities as their primary source of

TABLE 7.1   Where are the funded pension assets?
In the U.S.

COUNTRY	TOTAL PENSION ASSETS USD $BILLION	ASSETS/GDP RATIO %[7]
U.S.A.[1]	$22,480	121.1%
U.K.	$2,868	108.2%
Japan[2]	$2,808	59.4%
Australia	$1,583	126.0%
Canada	$1,575	102.8%
Netherlands	$1,296	168.3%
Switzerland[3]	$817	123.3%
South Korea	$575	40.9%
Germany[4]	$415	11.9%
Brazil[5]	$251	14.2%
South Africa	$207	73.8%
Finland	$199	83.2%
Malaysia	$190	62.7%
Chile	$172	73.0%
Mexico	$154	14.5%
Italy	$153	8.2%
France	$146	5.9%
China[6]	$141	1.2%
Hong Kong	$133	42.0%
Ireland	$130	42.2%
India	$105	4.7%
Spain	$39	3.1%
Total	**$36,436**	**62.0%[8]**

[1] U.S.A. assets include IRAs.
[2] Japan assets do not include the unfunded benefit obligation of corporate pension plans (account receivables).
[3] Switzerland assets only includes autonomous pension funds. Do not consider insurance companies assets.
[4] Germany assets only include pension assets for company pension schemes.
[5] Brazil assets only include pension assets from closed entities.
[6] China assets only include Enterprise Annuity assets.
[7] The Assets/GDP ratio for individual markets are calculated in local currency terms, and the total Assets/GDP ratio is calculated in USD.
[8] The ratio of Total Pension Assets to GDP declined from 2016 with the addition of China. China's pension assets represent 1.2% of total GDP.

Source: The 2017 Willis Towers Watson Global Pension Asset Study, 2017.

retirement savings. These products themselves are backed by investments in Europe's government bond markets, where acute pressure is being brought to bear as a result of sluggish economic growth, high unemployment, expanding deficits, and zero—or even negative—interest rates.

When the reforms we advocate in Workplace Savings 4.0 are adopted, our advantage in retirement finance will accelerate. Further action by Congress to ensure Social Security's long-term solvency could then vault the United States to a position of global leadership for success in providing citizens with retirement security.

Pay-as-you-go pension systems have no choice but to draw assets out of the productive economy and apply them immediately to meet current pension obligations. By contrast, DC systems gather assets through worker deferrals and channel them into investments that power the capital markets that drive the national economy. In the United States today, workplace savings plans now channel hundreds of billions a year into productive capital investment. And my sense is that nations that successfully mobilize the savings of their entire workforce, and direct those savings into dynamic securities markets, will enjoy a growing competitive advantage in the twenty-first century.

Governments around the world appreciate this dynamic. This is why so many of them are following the lead of the United States and Australia and scrambling to promote defined contribution workplace savings plans of their own. In this respect, the United States retirement finance system has a 20- to 40-year lead on other developed economies, most of which are just getting started on significantly growing their people's DC retirement savings.

This trend toward bolstering DC savings is quite strong across the world's seven largest pension markets—Australia, Canada, Japan, the Netherlands, Switzerland, the United Kingdom, and the United States—which account for nearly 92 percent of global retirement savings. Data from Willis Towers Watson's most recent global survey show that DC savings in these nations have been rising 5.6 percent a year for the past decade, well over twice as fast as the growth of traditional DB assets.

Many policy makers today clearly recognize that there are real and powerful advantages to shifting from DB to DC. All too often, traditional pension architecture can cause business, labor, and government to engage in a zero-sum competition for limited supplies of capital. In predominantly DC systems, all three tend to pull in the same direction, with government providing tax incentives through which workers save and invest capital for industry, and then, down the road, share in profits when they retire and draw down their savings.

That is why the U.S. DC retirement savings system has already had a strongly positive impact on U.S. savings and economic growth. As we will see in the next chapter, America's workplace savings system is not a drain on the economy the way pay-as-you-go systems are in much of the world. In fact, if we act to strengthen it and shore up its gaps, our DC system—401(k)s, IRAs, and the like—can support a virtuous circle of mass-based investment, economic growth, and broadly shared capital ownership, a "people's capitalism." Done right, the next generation of workplace savings can help us reboot economic growth and keep the American promise.

CHAPTER 8

WORKPLACE SAVINGS, CAPITAL MARKETS, AND ECONOMIC GROWTH

*Economists of every school have always recognized
savings as the source of investment that fuels
an economy's long-term growth. Nations
that have acted on this insight have gained
powerful competitive advantage over time.*
—Oxford Economics report, *Another Penny Saved*

For most of this book, we've talked about workplace retirement savings as a vehicle for producing reliable income for life. And while America does have substantial shortfalls to address, what we've just seen in the previous chapter shows that we are actually much better positioned than many other nations to reach this goal.

That's partly because our defined contribution workplace savings and IRAs are so huge—over $15 trillion and growing rapidly, notwithstanding ongoing cash-outs. But just as important as the volume of these assets is the nature of their ownership and how well they are allocated. And in all three of these respects, the United States is unique.

Defined benefit pension funds are owned by sponsoring entities and managed by fund trustees. Unless workers take lump-sum payouts instead of annuitized income (severing ties to the fund), all they really own in a DB plan is access to a promised income stream, not to the underlying assets that generate the wealth. And when pension funds find that they cannot meet their liabilities, as has too often been the case around the world in recent years, workers discover that the benefits they had expected to receive may not be there for them.

Workers in DC plans, by contrast, personally own the capital that they (or their advisors) can allocate into myriad investments, convert to annuitized income streams, or preserve to be passed on to their heirs or to charity. This is real ownership, a qualitatively different thing than a claim to a share of a traditional pension entitlement.

In terms of asset allocation, we have noted that most global pension funds are characterized by substantial fixed-income risk concentration, which, in an era of zero and even negative interest rates, raises any number of questions about retirement finance stability.

DC savings plans in the United States, however, are allocated to a wide variety of securities, which in part accounts for the speed with which they recovered in the post-financial crisis period. U.S. retirement assets fell sharply—by 22 percent—in the market dislocation of 2008. But they regained their 2007 peak by the end of 2010 and have been steadily increasing ever since.

U.S. workplace savings plans allow investors to directly participate in ownership of the private economy—through company stock, bonds, and other financial instruments. This may not be the "Pension Fund Socialism" that Peter Drucker forecast in the 1970s, but it is mass capitalism and worker ownership of the means of production, a new development that puts an interesting twist on the old idea of "class struggle."

In this chapter, I'd like to step back to see the issue of retirement finance in a much broader context than we typically do. That means looking deeper into the catalytic role that rising workplace savings have played in growing America's capital markets and the national economy.

Clearly, our capital markets generate returns that benefit workers in defined contribution plans. But this support system actually creates a virtuous circle. By providing vast, steady liquidity for stock and bond markets, 401(k)s, IRAs, and other retirement savings vehicles have become an essential source for American capital formation and helped the United States create a market-centered financing system that supplements, and surpasses, traditional commercial banking.

The Capital Markets System

Parallel with the rise of DC savings in recent decades, the United States has evolved a national financial system in which securities markets play a much larger role than traditional banks. We can see this by comparing U.S. and European financial models. In the European Union (for example, Britain), roughly 80 percent of corporate debt takes the form of bank loans, with just 20 percent of company finance coming from bond markets. In the United States, those proportions are reversed.

But nothing illustrates the difference in philosophy and financial architecture between the United States and other countries better than a comparison of equity markets and banks. While there are several individual countries around the world with robust stock exchanges, they are mostly outliers. In general, American companies are much more inclined to issue stock to secure a major share of their capital needs.

Comparing stock market capitalization and bank assets as a proportion of GDP shows that the United States is well over twice as "stock-intensive" as Europe, and that Japan is three times as "bank-intensive" as the United States (Figure 8.1). This discrepancy between stock market and bank intermediation also holds true when comparing the United States with the countries of the Organization of Economic Cooperation and Development (OECD), an intergovernmental body encompassing 35 of the world's largest economies with an aggregate GDP of $51 trillion. The United States is 40 percent more equity-intensive than the OECD; the OECD is 40 percent more bank-intensive than the United States.

The United States has vastly expanded all dimensions of its financial industry over recent decades, with this expansion paralleling the rise of funded pensions and workplace retirement savings. While the United States and the European Union are roughly the same size as economic entities (U.S. GDP is

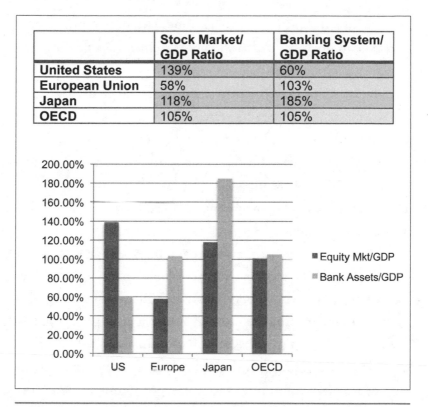

	Stock Market/ GDP Ratio	Banking System/ GDP Ratio
United States	139%	60%
European Union	58%	103%
Japan	118%	185%
OECD	105%	105%

FIGURE 8.1   Stock markets vs. banks: the U.S., EU, Japan, and OECD

Source: Federal Reserve economic data.

$18 trillion; the European Union's GDP is $19 trillion), U.S. stock and bond markets are nearly twice as large as their European counterparts: $62 trillion as compared with $35 trillion in Europe. United States banking assets are likewise much larger—$60 trillion as compared with $34 trillion in the European Union.

The sheer scale of America's financial system, and the fact that most world financial assets are priced and exchanged in U.S. dollars, provides deeper capital resources than most nations can imagine; it also allows for tremendous flexibility in times of systemic financial stress.

Following the 2008–2009 global financial crisis, for example, U.S. securities markets were buttressed by unprecedented central bank intervention when the Federal Reserve generated new liquidity, flattened interest rates, and quadrupled its balance sheet from $900 billion in the fall of 2008 to $3 trillion five years later, mostly by buying up fixed-income instruments and securitized debt.

This was clearly an extraordinary intervention, the reverberations of which are sure to play out over many years. We've already seen how the public-private hybrid structure of America's retirement finance—Social Security plus workplace savings—helps diversify risk. Similarly, our financial system as a whole benefits from a fairly well balanced twin-engine structure of its own, combining vast commercial and savings bank assets with even larger equity and bond markets.

After the 2008–2009 crisis, it took several years for the American financial system to stabilize and recover. But our stock of total retirement assets bounded back to their precrisis level by 2010. Today, our $26 trillion stock of retirement assets continues to grow by about 5 percent a year and our economy, employment, and wage growth are recovering more rapidly and on a more secure financial base than those of many key global rivals. The capital markets-driven U.S. economy was clearly gathering steam by the mid 2010s. But as of year-end 2016, the more heavily bank-centric financial systems of Europe and Asia were growing more slowly, and their traditional pension systems remained very much under a cloud.

This differential in recovery and economic growth can be credited largely to the extraordinary flexibility, dynamism, and sensitivity of America's capital market system, fueled as it is by steady flows of patient long-term capital from our workplace savings system.

Capital Markets and Banks

In any economic system, overall savings provide the funds to finance new business and real estate investments. But not all financial systems or forms of saving are created equal. The American capital market system, for example, has proven highly adept at capital formation generally, most especially in channeling capital into mechanisms that foster start-ups, innovation, and entrepreneurship such as angel investing, venture capital, and private equity.

These risk-seeking investors typically spread their bets among multiple ventures and entrepreneurial firms aiming to secure outsized returns from a standout success or two, while being able to wait out, or write off, multiple nonperformers. Every Google, Facebook, or Amazon emerges alongside hundreds of other start-ups that succeed on a more modest scale, get acquired by other firms, pivot to other strategies, or simply fail.

Unlike the capital markets, commercial banks can't play much of a role in financing start-up companies. By law, they must restrict their lending to well-established, creditworthy customers and avoid unproven, high-risk ventures. Banks can't collect outsized returns from successful clients. They are, however, very much exposed to the possible failure of any firm to which they lend money. But the ability to offset multiple losses with just a few out-sized gains is the key to financing entrepreneurship in America.

American retirement savers provide the market liquidity that enables entrepreneurs and their backers to incubate and launch new ideas. That's because when venture investors finance a start-up, they are looking forward to the day they can take that firm public with an initial public offering (IPO). And even if few retirement investors directly buy IPOs, U.S. equity markets are primed to embrace these new companies precisely because of the trillions of dollars in retirement savings that flow through them every year.

That's one reason why America's IPO market, while highly variable year to year, has averaged some $150 billion a year since the dawn of this new century. This influx of disruptive new competitors is, in large measure, why the lists of leading firms on the NYSE or NASDAQ change so much from decade to decade, while in Europe and Asia, established corporate brands dominate industry sectors for generations.

Even the failures among new businesses in the United States keep our economic system nimble. By introducing new ideas and business practices (such as online brokerage, alternative energy, mobile computing, and driverless vehicles), start-ups often force "incumbents" to stay sharp and innovate, or fade.

Many an S&P 500 company has opted to, in effect, "disrupt" itself by closing down mature, high-margin business lines in favor of emerging (and potentially larger) narrow-margin markets, all to avoid being pushed out of the way by energetic and well-funded start-ups. This has happened in wealth management and retirement savings throughout my career, where this process of industry reinvention is—if anything—accelerating.

Workplace Savings:
Fuel for Capital Markets

Some believe that economic dynamism and bold innovation are disruptive or destabilizing. And in less flexible, bank-centric financial systems, this may well be the case. But in the American system, while being displaced by upstart competitors isn't always comfortable for established firms, it is part and parcel of the creative destruction that serially razes and rebuilds corporate America, lifting the efficiency and productivity of the whole economy in the process.

This is how economic dynamism connects to, and depends on, robust workplace savings. In part because we have so many trillions in workplace savings absorbing mainstream equities and bonds, the United States also has the world's deepest market for alternative investments, with private equity, venture, real estate, and hedge funds worth some $3 trillion—fully half of all the alternative assets under management on earth.

While risk-engaging pension funds, endowments, sovereign wealth funds, and high-net-worth individuals are out investing in disruption, our workplace retirement system deploys assets in a less glamorous but equally vital way, investing in every corner of our stock and bond markets with long-term patient capital, staying in place for decades and forming the bedrock of America's capital markets.

This synergy between retirement savings and American capital markets has been growing for decades. By channeling vast sums of money from many millions of workplace savers into our capital markets, America's workplace saving system has become central to our whole economy's growth (Figure 8.2).

153

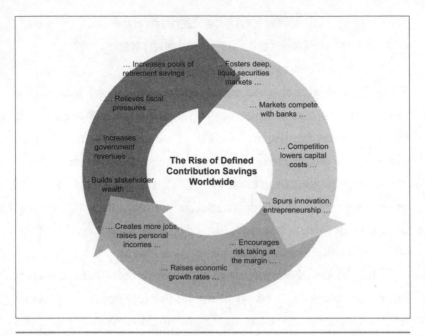

FIGURE 8.2 Retirement savings can fuel capital market growth in what becomes a virtuous circle

Source: Lenny Glynn.

Decades of Growth

Since the passage of ERISA in 1974, DB pension funds and the newer DC plans that emerged to supplant them have driven wave after wave of savings into U.S. capital markets. America's total stock market capitalization, for example, has surged from some $700 billion in 1975 to over $25 trillion today. As a share of the overall economy, stock valuation has grown from 40 percent of U.S. GDP to 146 percent of GDP over the same period.

When you compare the rising market capitalization of American stock markets with total U.S. retirement savings over the years, it's clear that these two systems have been marching in near lockstep in a virtuous circle. This is no coincidence: U.S. retirement assets are fueling the stock market, and a rising stock market is driving up U.S. retirement assets.

This remarkable form of mutually supportive retirement savings capitalism has not yet been achieved in any other country—with the possible exception of Australia, which has a mandatory national savings system to which all workers must contribute at least 9 percent of their salaries. This has given Australia the highest level of per capita managed assets of any country.

The ratio of total stock market value to national GDP is often used as a rough proxy to measure the difference in capital market "intensity" between the United States and the rest of the world. One glance shows that stock markets play a much greater role in the U.S. economy than they do in the world as a whole. This is because U.S. equity markets have been infused with trillions of dollars in savings by tens of millions of working people, while most other developed country retirement systems still rely primarily on tax flows into pay-as-you-go structures that may transfer payments directly to retirees without those funds ever being productively invested. Few other countries have anything remotely comparable to the way American workers' savings flow into our capital markets and help our economy grow (Figure 8.3).

Just as U.S. retirement savings and capital markets rose together, the absence of a well-funded retirement system in other developed countries means that their capital markets too remain relatively underdeveloped (Figure 8.4). Without access to the massive investment flows generated by funded pensions

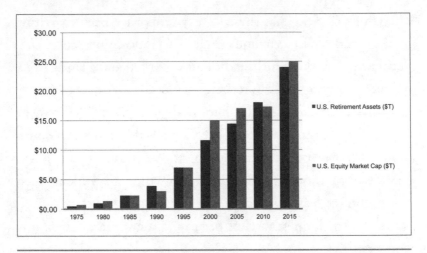

FIGURE 8.3 U.S. retirement assets and U.S. equity market cap

Sources: Investment Company Institute, Federal Reserve, and World Bank.

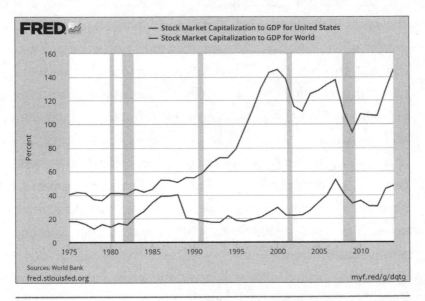

FIGURE 8.4 U.S. and world equity markets/GDP

Sources: Investment Company Institute, Federal Reserve, and World Bank.

and workplace retirement savings, most other countries effectively starve their capital markets of investment liquidity, leaving their economies overwhelmingly dependent on rigid, risk-averse bank lending.

Let's recall that U.S.-funded pension assets account for fully two-thirds of the $36 trillion in retirement assets controlled by the world's top 22 pension markets. The U.S. system of funded retirement finance, at $26 trillion, is about 10 times the size of Japan's, the second largest market. And in Japan, as in many other markets, pension assets are primarily invested in government debt, exposing savers to highly concentrated sovereign risk. U.S. retirement assets, on the other hand, are a masterpiece of diversification, with tens of millions of individual portfolios allocated across innumerable stocks, bonds, mutual funds, and other instruments.

Expanded Savings and the U.S. Economy

This tight relationship between retirement savings, U.S. capital markets, and economic innovation and growth makes it clear that the Workplace Savings 4.0 reforms we explored in Chapter 6 would do far more than just provide additional financial assets for American retirees. By engaging tens of millions more American workers in capital market investing, these reforms would generate trillions of dollars in new flows into our capital markets and produce strong tailwinds for future economic growth.

According to estimates by EBRI, the Workplace Savings 4.0 reforms we described would inject an additional $700 billion annually into workplace savings plans, accelerating their annual growth by fully 10 percent, from 5 percent to 5.5 percent. By 2025, this would, in turn, inject an extra $5 trillion into overall workplace savings, raising projected assets from $33 to $38 trillion.

To gauge the economic impact that higher savings rates in the United States could have, Putnam Investments, together with the U.S. Chamber of Commerce, AARP, the Aspen Institute, the American Society of Pension Professionals & Actuaries (ASPPA), and other financial industry partners, cosponsored a 2014 study by the consultancy Oxford Economics entitled "Another Penny Saved: The Economic Benefits of Higher U.S. Savings."

As the title of the study suggests, the results showed that even small adjustments in savings behavior by tens of millions of workers across a system as large as the U.S. workplace savings market can have a profound long-term impact.

Using data from EBRI, the report's authors found that America's savings gap was centered primarily on lower-income individuals and families, particularly the lowest income quartile, where savings would have to increase by about 21 percent of pretax income to achieve economic and retirement security. This demographic group is made up mainly of people who most often lack access to any form of workplace savings plan. Closing that coverage gap is, of course, Workplace Savings 4.0's top policy priority.

Besides extending savings coverage to as many workers as possible, the Oxford study also recommended that all existing savings incentives and vehicles should be preserved and made more effective through the near-universal adoption of fully automatic plan design and significantly higher savings rates.

The report drew a close parallel between long-term individual economic security and long-term national economic prosperity and urged that public policy never pit personal solvency against national solvency in a misguided quest for fiscal savings. This is precisely the counterproductive push-and-pull between governments, corporations, and individuals competing for scarce capital that we mentioned in the last chapter.

Those of us working in the retirement savings industry have always known that retirement savings were a critical source of liquidity for America's capital markets. With total DC plan and IRA assets worth $15 trillion and expanding, net of redemptions, by more than $850 billion a year, how could this not be the case? But the report confirmed what many of us had long believed—that a strong, steady flow of personal retirement savings plays a vital role in the health of the national economy as a whole.

Mobilizing their working population's assets to finance investment can thus be a critical source of competitive advantage for any nation that gets savings policy right.

"Another Penny Saved" suggests that the optimal, healthy range of investment for the U.S. economy is in the range of 20 to 25 percent of GDP. But despite the growth we've seen in workplace retirement savings plans, Americans' personal savings rate has slipped from about 14 percent of disposable income in 1980 to about 5 percent today.

So the United States has had to look abroad for much of its economic fuel in recent decades, borrowing extensively from nations with higher savings rates and selling off a substantial share of our own assets to foreign investors. American house-holds' ownership of nonfinancial capital market assets has declined from over 80 percent in 1970 to 60 percent today. Over the same period, foreign investors' share rose from 3 per-cent to 20 percent. (Foreign flows accelerated in the years after the global financial crisis as investors scrambled to acquire safer, U.S.-dollar-denominated assets.)

This means we have some real work to do. But the Oxford study suggests that if we could boost the overall investment level in the economy to an average of 22.5 percent, with that rise funded by higher household savings, we could increase Ameri-ca's projected 2040 GDP by around 3 percent, a gain equal to an additional net present value of $7 trillion, roughly 40 per-cent of today's annual GDP.

This expanded savings would generate greater household wealth, accelerate national economic growth, and, by reducing our dependence on foreign investors, better insulate U.S. capi-tal markets from international capital shocks.

The Ownership Society

American workers already have a significant stake in financial assets, and an interest in public policies that foster economic growth on new business formations. And as the wages-to-wealth mechanism of retirement savings deepens and broadens to cover nearly all American workers, it will take us even fur-ther toward becoming an ownership society.

The mere fact of having any savings or real assets at all offers a wide array of positive benefits to individuals, families, and society as a whole. Multiple studies have shown, for example, that ownership of even a small amount of financial assets can have a significant effect. Low- and moderate-income students with even low levels of savings set aside for college are three times more likely to enroll in college and four times more likely to graduate than students with no savings at all. These positive effects work even for families who didn't send their children to college, but who do have some assets saved.

To link family aspirations to the power of America's financial markets, elected officials have proposed legislation that would establish universal child savings accounts or "baby accounts" that would set every newborn on the road to a lifetime of savings and asset creation.

We've also seen proposals for expanded child tax credits that would incentivize families to save for their children. On reaching age 21, young people could use this money to pay for college, make a down payment on a home, or roll it over into a Roth IRA. Either way, this universal approach would provide every American child a first step down the road toward personal development and financial self-reliance, with important secondary effects for our society.

Wealth inequality is much in the news of late. Many seem to believe that our country is dividing into two Americas, one with financial assets and one without. Worse, the policies used to stabilize financial markets in recent years haven't directly benefited Americans who don't own financial assets. And those outside the system are increasingly frustrated by this inequality of financial opportunity.

This is unacceptable. But the most powerful tool that we can deploy to address this wealth disparity isn't the *redistribution* of wealth via the tax code, but concerted private/public collaboration in the *creation* of financial assets for all Americans.

Giving everyone an opportunity to take a personal stake in the continuing growth of U.S. capital markets would be a major economic, social, and political step forward. We need to ensure that all citizens have a real, tangible stake in free enterprise so that they support pro-growth public policies. Then we need the policies to make the growth happen.

CHAPTER 9

SIGNS OF THINGS TO COME

*Change is the law of life. Those who look only to
the past or present are certain to miss the future.*
—JOHN F. KENNEDY

M ost of this book describes the remarkable evolution of
the workplace savings system that I have witnessed over
the course of my career, together with a look at where I believe
we're headed if we enact the reforms we've advocated in Workplace Savings 4.0. But if we cast our gaze just a little further,
we can already see emerging demographic, social, political, and
market trends that foretell dramatic improvements to, and
expansion of, our private retirement system.

Taken together, these trends promise quite good news—
broader coverage, greater worker engagement, adaptation to
emerging economic trends, and the embrace of new financial
technologies that dramatically improve plan quality while continuing to lower costs. Taken together, they will give rise to a
markedly superior workplace savings system. And they also
promise real gains on broad economic challenges like wealth

inequality, capital formation, and economic growth. We've come a long way, and we're about to move ahead by leaps and bounds. Here are some signs of things to come.

The Millennials Shall Inherit the Earth

The millennials are taking over. While 10,000 boomers turn 65 every day, the 75.4 million millennials (born between 1982 and 2004) have just surpassed the 74.9 million boomers to become the largest generation in our history.

By almost any measure, the millennial generation will prove historic. They are, collectively, the best-educated generation ever. They will likely become the wealthiest and longest-lived as well. And the experience of millennials will ultimately prove the utility of our workplace retirement savings system.

First off, most will spend their entire career in defined contribution workplace savings programs. Many boomers began their careers in the DB world and then were moved into DC plans in stages over the past generation. As a result, many retiring boomers will have spent only a fraction of their careers accumulating retirement savings in workplace plans. By contrast, most millennials will spend their entire careers saving through on-the-job payroll deduction.

Second, millennials will have better and less costly retirement savings plans. Millennials will never experience the suboptimal plan designs of Workplace Savings 1.0 and 2.0. Instead, they will spend their careers in more advanced Workplace Savings 3.0 plans (and, I hope, in the Workplace Savings 4.0 designs now emerging).

This means they will benefit from auto-enrollment, auto-escalation, and guidance to post-Pension Protection Act "default" options—typically, target date funds (TDFs) and managed accounts. And they will take advantage of new financial technologies such as cloud computing, asset allocation algorithms, and mobile apps, all of which drive costs down and quality up.

Even the global financial crisis of 2008–2009 seems to have had at least one thin silver lining. Multiple wealth management industry surveys suggest that the downturn actually inspired millennials to focus intently on their own retirement savings. Today, over 70 percent of millennials are already saving.

And millennials don't seem to mind a firm "nudge" in the right direction. A survey done by Natixis shows 82 percent of millennials think employers should be required to offer retirement plans. More surprisingly, fully 69 percent of millennials (as compared with 55 percent of boomers) think retirement savings should be mandatory for individual workers.

Critically, they are getting into gear on saving for retirement early in their careers. According to the Investment Company Institute, the median age at which boomers began purchasing mutual funds was in their thirties, and for generation X (born between the mid-1960s and the early 1980s) the median age was 27. But millennials began buying mutual funds at age 23.

This may prove to be the best news of all because the three most important factors for accumulating retirement assets—the amount saved, the duration of savings across worker careers, and the allocation of savings into risk-managed glide paths—are all totally within investors' control.

On the other side of the ledger, millennials are contending with negative pressures that weighed far less on earlier generations. These include over a trillion dollars in student loans, soaring healthcare costs, credit card debt, flattening wage growth, and steeply rising real estate valuations that make it harder for millennials to take their first steps on the property ladder.

As of 2016, U.S. home ownership, at 63.6 percent, was at its lowest level in 50 years, down from over 69 percent prior to the 2008–2009 financial crisis. This drop in home ownership is almost entirely due to the financial travails of millennials, who also face stiff competition and high prices for rental housing.

So while the retirement savings industry is clearly offering superior products and services at steadily falling prices, the need to pay for healthcare, education, and housing all crimp millennials' ability to save. Continuing economic recovery and an improving job market could help mitigate this challenge, especially if it leads to higher wages that could enable greater retirement saving.

Longer term, though, millennials stand to inherit the earth—or at least $30 trillion of it. That's *trillion* with a capital *T*.

For decades, boomers have been busy acquiring substantial real estate and socking away over $15 trillion in DC retirement savings and IRA savings. According to the consulting firm Accenture, boomers will pass down $30 trillion to their millennial and generation X children.

So American millennials may have it tough now. But they stand to benefit from the greatest intergenerational wealth transfer in the history of money. DC workplace savings plans will play an important role since they allow workers to accumulate substantial wealth that can be *inherited*, unlike DB plans, which only provide an income stream until a retiree dies.

This cascade of wealth will be unequally concentrated, and some millennials will benefit far more than others. This very predictable disparity may be the best argument for expanding both the depth and breadth of workplace defined contribution savings coverage.

If the U.S. economy grows, and if our workplace retirement savings system is expanded to cover nearly all American workers, then the even greater intergenerational wealth transfer to come—when the millennials eventually pass assets on to their children and grandchildren—will not only be larger by an order of magnitude, but will be shared by a much broader cross-section of American families.

Closing the Coverage Gap

No question about it, we have a retirement coverage gap. Roughly half of American workers who work at small firms—some 50 million, mostly working at small firms or self-employed—have no savings option on the job. Any meaningful solution to this challenge should be comprehensive—offering a payroll savings option to every worker who pays Social Security tax.

For some time, a bipartisan group of retirement policy experts and legislators has sought to do just this by giving workers without access to 401(k)s and other ERISA-approved DC plans access to an automatic-enrollment IRA, an Auto-IRA. This idea gathered momentum in the optimistic period after passage of the landmark Pension Protection Act in 2006 but lost speed amid the mandate fatigue in the wake of the Affordable Care Act.

In response, several U.S. states—notably Illinois, California, Maryland, Connecticut, and my home state of Massachusetts—took up the idea themselves. As of this writing, some two dozen states are at some stage of developing new workplace Auto-IRAs that would be sponsored by state governments and managed by private investment firms.

All of these plans are universal. Virtually all employers would be obliged to offer either one of these plans or a traditional DC plan. Employees would be free to opt out. And all would offer automatic enrollment—the critical mechanism, proven over a generation, for steeply increasing worker participation. So far, so good.

But these plans are seriously flawed. They generally propose default contribution rates in the range of 3 percent—too low by half. While some proposed plans would default workers into target date funds, others have suggested more conservative allocations unlikely to provide sufficient returns. And most would limit expenses to between 0.5 percent and 1 percent, which is not egregious, but certainly no bargain for a bare-bones plan. (According to the Investment Company Institute, 401(k) plan participants pay just 0.48 percent on average for equity mutual funds.)

The idea of offering broader access to workplace retirement savings plans is of course laudable. But the proposed patchwork quilt state government-sponsored plans raise a number of questions.

- They suggest a two-tier system in which employees of large firms enjoy state-of-the-art ERISA plans, while workers at small firms (where new jobs are increasingly created) are relegated to stripped-down plans beyond the reach of ERISA protections and best practices.

- There is concern that the state plans might erode our successful private retirement savings system by encouraging small employers that might otherwise offer private ERISA-compliant 401(k) plans to opt for lower-quality state-sponsored options.
- It's fair to ask why the emerging state plans are being granted an exemption from ERISA regulations while substantially similar private workplace savings plans are not. Simple principles of fair play suggest that payroll deduction programs administered by states should compete on a level playing field with private savings programs.
- Since some of these emerging state plans may include various forms of guaranteed income, state and local governments, already struggling with a multitrillion-dollar pension funding gap, might find themselves on the hook for billions more.
- Finally, there is the perennial question of economies of scale. A national Auto-IRA system would almost certainly deliver better quality at lower costs, avoiding what Alicia Munnell, director of the Boston College Center for Retirement Research, has called the "laborious, time-consuming, and expensive process of setting up 50 different plans."

But do we really need government plan sponsorship? Many industry experts believe that it would be simpler, cheaper, and more efficient to offer workplace savings through new private plan structures aimed specifically at small business.

One leading proposal, long buoyed by bipartisan support, would be to expand access for small employers and their employees to multiple employer plans (MEPs) that would enroll employees from hundreds or thousands of small firms, even including self-employed contingent workers.

For many years, MEPs have been used to sponsor 401(k) offerings for closely related organizations like trade and professional associations. But small firms outside these industry groups have lacked access. MEPs would allow small employers without the ability to administer their own plans to enroll their employees into professionally managed workplace plans that offer all the best practices and administrative economies of scale found in the 401(k) plans of large companies.

This would, in turn, offer the small-firm employees who today struggle to save in their own IRAs everything we have come to associate with Workplace Savings 3.0—auto-enrollment, auto-escalation, and automatic allocation to TDFs and managed accounts. MEPs would also allow for employer matches and give workers the opportunity to save up to $18,000 per year as compared to the $5,500 allowed by 2016 IRA limits.

MEPs offer employees a workplace savings experience that is qualitatively superior to the plans contemplated by the states, at equal or less cost. The prospect of potentially dozens of new state-level plans should be a wake-up call to the retirement services industry and to Congress to get to work on Auto-IRAs and MEPs in order to extend the benefits of our private savings system to small-business, lower-income workers, and the emerging freelancers and consultants of the "gig economy." It seems only right that we extend the coverage of our ERISA-regulated workplace savings system through national solutions open to as many American workers as possible.

Contingent Workers and the "Gig Economy"

One of the greatest strengths of the defined contribution workplace savings model is its extraordinary flexibility and portability. Over the decades, as job tenures grew progressively shorter and the number of jobs per career increased, DC plans allowed workers to pick up and take their tax-incented savings with them. Economists routinely cite this labor flexibility and dynamism as a critical asset of business in the United States.

But the latest round of employment evolution—contingent labor and the gig economy—has thrown a wrench into our plans for next-generation savings plans. After all, what good is a Workplace Savings 4.0 savings plan for workers who are outside the formal workplace?

While the use of freelancers, short-term temporary workers, contractors, and self-employed entrepreneurs has been growing for years, it really took off after the Great Recession of 2008–2009. The year 2015 saw the fastest year-over-year increase in the number of new freelance entrepreneurs in two decades. According to some estimates, by 2020, some 40 percent of the workforce—60 million workers—may be freelancers, contractors, or temp workers.

The challenge is to offer the benefits of a more perfect workplace savings system to every kind of worker. We need to find ways to give these gig economy workers, who already pay *double* into Social Security, the opportunity to save on the job without the payroll support of a full-time employer. Certainly this growing sector of the workforce deserves something as simple as access to a savings plan.

Individual tax credits to match contributions could help incentivize workers to enroll in retirement savings plans. Congress may consider providing matching tax credits—perhaps 50 percent up to the first $1,000 saved—to encourage young contract workers to get started.

To reach workers beyond the traditional workplace, we should engage them with the kind of cloud-based mobile apps that have become ubiquitous. To effectively communicate, educate, and support transactions, let's take a page out of Uber's playbook and create an easy, frictionless retirement savings vehicle where independent workers can engage an advisor online and arrange for a percentage of their income, from any employer, anytime they get paid, to be automatically diverted to a retirement savings account.

This digital plan design should include all of the automatic features seen in traditional payroll deduction plans, together with behavioral finance "nudges" that tell savers when it's time to act and encourage choices that ensure adequate savings deferrals. In the twenty-first-century economy, the pace of working, saving, and spending is accelerating. We need to act now to create savings options that support the nontraditional worker in an increasingly nontraditional workplace.

The World's Largest DC Plan May Soon Reach GI Joe and Jane

The $458 billion Thrift Savings Plan (TSP) is by far the world's largest workplace DC savings plan, and arguably one of the best. The fund offers federal government civilian employees automatic enrollment at a 3 percent deferral (this should be higher!) in low-cost funds with minimal administrative fees subsidized by the agencies for which they work. While the plan is sponsored by government agencies, it is managed and administered by the private asset management industry.

The TSP offers a lean, streamlined set of just five funds—a U.S. government debt fund, a fixed-income investment, a common stock index fund, a small-cap stock index fund, and an international stock index fund—together with target date options constructed from these core funds.

And the TSP may soon grow substantially. Today, members of the armed services have only a traditional DB plan which, while generous, only delivers for "lifers"—the 20 percent of enlisted personnel and 50 percent of officers who complete a full 20-year vesting period. Most men and women in uniform accrue no DB retirement benefits whatsoever. TSP options for members of the uniformed services are strictly limited to deferrals from designated special pay, incentive pay, and bonuses. But in the near future, retirement finance for our military may change dramatically.

Like private employers, the U.S. military wants a nimble, flexible workforce. Rather than maintain an expensive standing army, the military needs to staff up or down in accordance with need. And, as with the private sector, a flexible and portable DC system may be the best way to achieve this.

As a result, the Department of Defense is contemplating a blended retirement system with reduced DB benefits and a new DC plan roughly in line with leading private sector workplace DC offerings like the TSP or private sector 401(k)s. The new system would provide service members with retirement assets equal to or greater than the current DB-only plan. And it would be very large.

Assuming an 87 percent participation rate (as with the existing TSP), the new military DC plan could *double* existing annual TSP inflows. That's good news for our service members and their families, and good news for the financial markets.

Convergence: DC plans, DB outcomes

Private sector retirement finance has been shifting from defined benefit to defined contribution for over a generation. While this evolution is often described as a shift of risk from plan sponsors to plan participants, the reality is more complex.

DC plans are continuously evolving. A new trend emerging in recent years is the inclusion in DC workplace plans of lifetime income provisions that mimic the annuitized income streams more typically seen in DB plans. Specifically, this means DC workplace plans can offer participants the option to invest some of their payroll deductions to secure the types of lifetime income streams delivered by DB plans. As this trend gathers steam, it promises to do much to mitigate the notion of DC plans as risky and replicate the certainty of traditional pensions.

At the same time, many firms have opted to convert their defined benefit plans into cash balance plans. These are technically DB plans, but they are managed on an individual account basis, like DC plans. Cash balance plans are, however, required to offer life annuities with benefits guaranteed by the Pension Benefit Guaranty Corporation. But many workers choose just to take the cash.

Roughly half of DB plan providers also offer their employees the option of cashing out their future income benefits and
taking a one-time lump sum. Aon Hewitt studies show that
most workers actually prefer cash now to income later—either
because they're not sure how long they may live or they are concerned that employers may renege on paying lifetime benefits.

All of these options—DC, cash balance, and DB—leave
many employees owning and managing substantial assets that
they eventually need to convert into income. So a retirement
finance system long perceived as bifurcated between DB and
DC models is, in fact, converging, obliging workers to plan for
and manage their income in retirement.

Over the long term, retirement savers who purchase some
form of guaranteed lifetime income—annuities, guaranteed
asset drawdown schemes, or deferred income annuities that pay
out in later old age (say at age 80 or beyond)—stand to benefit by ensuring income in late old age. This is no sure thing
for those that self-manage their assets without guarantees. The
more we can do to encourage workers to choose at least some
guaranteed income choice, in plan and beyond, the better.

Evolving Allocation Strategies—Target Date Funds and Managed Accounts

When target date funds (TDFs) emerged in the mid-1990s,
they offered an investment option with advice effectively baked
in. By selecting a single future retirement (or target) date, a
retirement saver could invest in a dynamic portfolio that began
with a weighted exposure to high-risk, high-return stocks,

then gradually shifted—without the investor needing to take action—to more conservative bonds and even cash as the retirement target date approached.

Rising workplace savings plans created a vast market for TDFs by the turn of the new millennium, and this demand accelerated dramatically with the passage of the Pension Protection Act of 2006. The PPA recognized TDFs as one of four qualified default investment alternatives (QDIAs)—along with stable value money market funds, balanced funds, and managed accounts—for plan sponsors who chose to offer automatic enrollment.

Since then, TDFs have become the hands-down favorite for plan sponsors and workplace savers. Fully 88.2 percent of QDIA assets now flow into TDFs, with money market funds coming in a distant second at 4.2 percent. Managed accounts, so far, have played a smaller and declining role. One industry survey stated that between 2013 and 2016, managed accounts shrank from just under 5 percent of the workplace market to the low single digits.

But the best days for managed accounts may yet lie ahead. The 22 percent annual surge in TDF assets since the adoption of the PPA—from $116 billion in 2006 to $880 billion by the end of 2016—seems to suggest that they will dominate future retirement savings. But that's by no means inevitable.

For one thing, not all TDFs are created equal. Even among those aiming at identical retirement dates, there are wide variances in allocations among stocks, bonds, and cash along the glide path. Some TDFs are designed to just go "to" retirement, producing a final allocation portfolio at the target date. Others go "through" their target date, maintaining a substantial allocation to stocks and then gradually reducing risk in the years after retirement. Debate between "to" and "through" proponents can be intense—and arcane. But one thing is clear: In the 2008–2009 financial crash, TDF owners with large equity positions close to their target dates experienced far more volatility than they had expected.

It also turns out that most TDFs have been neither leaders in investment innovation nor outperformers. Large endowment funds, for example, now invest over 50 percent of their holdings in nontraditional asset classes like real estate, commodities, and various hedging strategies. State pension funds put 25 percent of their assets into these alternatives. But TDFs are still 95 percent allocated to traditional long-only stock and bonds.

In terms of investment returns, in the decade from 2003 to 2013, endowments returned 8.2 percent per year, and state pension funds returned 7.2 percent, while TDFs returned only 6.3 percent—a bit lower than returns from a simple 60/40 stock/bond allocation.

But the toughest challenge ahead for TDFs could be that their basic selling point may no longer be valid. For much of the past century, stocks and bonds were negatively correlated. This meant that retirement savings portfolios could manage risk by rotating allocations from equities to bonds as workers approached retirement.

But since the late 1990s, stock and bond market movements have been more highly correlated, especially in the low-interest-rate environment that has followed the global financial crisis. This undercuts the historic diversification benefits of investing in fixed-income assets late in the glide path, as retirement nears.

So despite the huge growth in TDFs, many retirement planners have begun exploring better ways to manage their clients' investment risk. Innovations based on behavioral finance theory, and falling costs for developing financial algorithms and allocation models, suggest that a new wave of innovation may be gaining enough traction to challenge TDF dominance in the same way that TDFs edged out other models from the 1990s forward.

Fine-tuned, cost-efficient managed accounts may soon be coming into their own. While managed accounts today comprise only a small fraction of the market for QDIAs, more than 50 percent of workplace plans offer managed accounts today. And while managed accounts have traditionally been aimed at investors with higher account balances, new technologies and efficiencies are today making them cost-efficient for a far broader market.

Unlike TDFs, which offer a single allocation strategy to thousands of workplace savers, managed accounts can actually tailor strategies to an individual's financial situation. They can, for example, take into account assets held outside the plan, a potential inheritance, real estate income, or other individually unique assets and liabilities. The result is a retirement savings strategy that optimizes accumulation and drawdown in accordance with unique individual requirements. In effect, next-generation managed accounts bring the "mass customization" that has become ubiquitous in e-commerce to the retirement and wealth management arenas.

This doesn't mean that managed accounts will replace TDFs anytime soon. For example, younger investors mostly share a similar goal—simply to build assets. So they may find that target date funds provide a perfectly adequate, low-cost option when they're just getting started.

But as workers' careers and their financial lives grow more complex, they may need a more precisely targeted managed account that takes into consideration variables such as outside assets, the state of the person's health, expected Social Security benefits, marital status, and other circumstances.

The idea of workplace savers making a pivot between TDFs and managed accounts has been termed a "dynamic QDIA." This suggests participants may automatically be guided to standard TDFs early in their careers and then, once a predetermined set of criteria is met, be offered managed accounts that provide more personalized investment and advisory services.

Another driver behind managed accounts is that they are not limited, as TDFs are, to providing investment allocations. They also provide *product* allocations beyond mutual funds and ETFs, including customized solutions for guaranteed retirement income.

By leveraging sophisticated risk models and allocation algorithms, and by extending into the drawdown phase of investing, managed accounts may more precisely (and personally) solve the complex challenges of later-stage working lives and improve retirement savings outcomes. If this concept evolves as I expect, managed accounts will begin to play a much greater role for older workers. But they won't supplant TDFs; rather, they will complement and, indeed, complete them.

Starting at the Beginning: Birthright Retirement Accounts

The savings that anyone can accumulate to generate income in retirement depends on just three variables—total savings, investment returns, and, most critically, time itself. How much money does a person save? How long has that money been set aside? And what has been the return on the investments?

This book has offered multiple policy ideas to help raise savings rates and improve returns through better asset allocation. But America's current retirement systems, both public and private, simply don't capture the full value of time itself. We leave 20+ years of compounding on the table.

That's because Social Security's benefit credits don't start until a person goes to work and pays FICA taxes. The same lost time limits returns to workplace savings. Most Americans, in other words, don't begin to accumulate any retirement savings until they enter the workforce in their twenties. Many wait even longer to get going. Sadly, some never save at all.

But there is a simple, powerful, and affordable way that we could turn the time value of money to the advantage of future generations. We could simply grant each newborn child a "birthright" retirement account of $1,000—and forbid them from touching it until they reach age 70 or die. As these babies grew up, they would, of course, be free to add funds to their birthright accounts and leave them to heirs if they died before age 70.

With fewer than 4 million babies born each year in the United States, funding these accounts from general tax revenues would cost about $4 billion a year, roughly one-tenth of 1 percent of Uncle Sam's $3.5 trillion-plus annual budget. Surely, this cost would be manageable.

Think of it, as I do, as a proactive rebate to future taxpayers. After all, the four million American babies born any given year will, as a group, pay trillions of dollars in federal taxes over their lifetimes. It seems chintzy for their Uncle Sam not to give them a head start on those obligations.

The financial, social, and psychological benefits that Americans would reap from birthright accounts would be enormous.

To start with, we'd be seeding an "ownership society" in which every American owns a piece of our free enterprise economy. And every penny in these accounts would be one less penny that an individual would have to claim from means-tested government programs like Medicaid in old age. The savings to the government, as future generations age, would be substantial.

Let's assume that the Social Security Administration, with U.S. Treasury or Federal Reserve oversight, would administer these accounts. Investment management could be bid out to private firms that could take full advantage of a *70-year investment horizon*. Investment choices would be limited to low-cost, risk-managed target date funds. What might the returns be?

At 6 percent—a fairly conservative estimate—$1,000 at birth would grow to nearly $66,000 by age 70 (Figure 9.1). And remember, nearly all of that money would have to be drawn down before the account owner could seek coverage by means-tested public benefit programs. Suppose this baby's parents decide to add just $500 a year to this account until age five. In that case, a 6 percent return would produce $204,000 by age 70—even more if the child put more into the account later in life. Those are impressive numbers.

But the social benefits would almost surely be even more impressive. Saving is not just about money, it's the seed corn of larger hopes and dreams. Multiple studies show that children of families who have *any savings at all* are more likely to finish school, form stable families, find work, stay off drugs and out of jail, and generally be more productive citizens. My guess is that these birthright accounts would "pay for themselves" many times over—creating wealth in American communities that today have literally no financial assets.

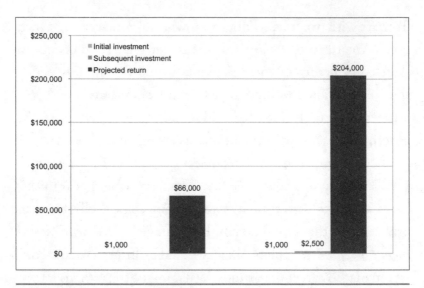

FIGURE 9.1 What "birthright" accounts could return by age 70: 70-year projection, earning 6% returns*

* The values assume monthly compounding so the effective rate of return is 6.17%.
Source: Putnam Investments estimates.

Let me close this little thought experiment with a simple reflection. So long as America remains an essentially compassionate society, we are committed to making sure our elders don't starve, go homeless, or die early for lack of medical care. That costs money. Serious money.

Today, we channel almost all that money to needy elders at the back-end of life—through tax-revenues from current workers. Maybe we should think seriously about beginning at the beginning. Doesn't it make sense to invest more of that money as early as possible to help children and young people at the front end of their lives? Can't we find ways to make time and compounding help our fellow citizens achieve greater self-reliance and enjoy the dignity of meeting their own needs?

I'm just asking. You answer.

CHAPTER 10

OPPORTUNITY AND RISK: TAX REFORM 2017?

Be careful what you wish for.
—Folk wisdom of unknown origin

As this book was heading to publication, developments in Washington, D.C., promised to have major impact—for good or ill—on America's retirement savings system. For the first time since 1986, a sweeping reform of the entire U.S. tax code began to seem possible—this time with Republicans in charge of the House, the Senate, and the White House.

For those of us involved in retirement policy, the opening of this kind of rare "window" for comprehensive tax reform is both exhilarating and unnerving. It's exciting because adopting more robust, better-designed tax incentives could go far toward actually "solving" America's whole retirement savings challenge—once and for all.

But sweeping tax reform is also fraught with risks—largely because of Congress's long-proven propensity to treat retirement savings incentives as a source of "pay-fors" for other tax cuts. Generally speaking, when politicians propose new tax cuts, they sift through existing tax deductions or deferrals to choose ones that they can reduce or eliminate so as to make other tax cuts revenue-neutral. Recent history, sadly, tells us that this search for "pay-fors" to offset individual and corporate tax reductions may again put retirement savings incentives at risk.

Tax Reform and Retirement Savings: 1986 and 2014

Retirement professionals grow cautious when major tax reform becomes a real possibility because we have seen this movie before—and watched as retirement savings got the short end of the stick.

The last truly comprehensive efforts—including the **Tax Reform Act of 1986**—dramatically simplified the tax code, broadened the base, and eliminated a clutter of tax shelters. But because Congress—in the spirit of Reagan— sought to achieve revenue neutrality in this legislation, the law also severely restricted the use of Individual Retirement Accounts (IRAs). While still allowing employees not covered by a pension plan to contribute the lesser of $2,000 or 100 percent of earned income, the law severely restricted IRA tax deductions for households (employee or spouse) that had either pension coverage or moderate to high incomes. The result was to seriously stall what had been the very rapid rise of IRA savings by America's mass affluent. It took years—and some further legislative tweaks—for the IRA market to recover.

Workplace savings had another close call a generation later when House Ways and Means Committee Chairman

Dave Camp of Michigan rolled out his **Tax Reform Act of 2014**, which would also have simplified the tax code, lowered corporate and individual tax rates, and reformed international tax rules. All worthy goals.

But to lower those rates, Camp's bill would also have cut roughly $250 billion in retirement savings incentives over the next decade and lowered the cap on how much savings in IRAs and K-plans could enjoy pretax treatment by roughly half. Further contributions would have to be after-tax contributions—as in the "Roth" savings accounts named for former Delaware Senator William V. Roth. The potential results would have been unpredictable, but most likely negative for overall savings rates.

As it happened, Camp's legislation—the product of years of hard bargaining and staff work—was undercut sharply right at its rollout, when then-Speaker John Boehner famously dismissed it as, "blah, blah, blah." But while it never passed into law, as of mid-2017, the "Camp Draft" is back in consideration and may yet play a role in guiding any comprehensive tax reform in 2017 or 2018. If so, that could put retirement savings incentives at risk—yet again.

The fate of workplace savings plans is so deeply entwined with tax reform because of the central role that tax incentives play in spurring nearly all retirement savings. For any nation, its tax code embodies key economic and political priorities, effectively defining the "financial DNA" of entire economies. This is certainly true in the United States—whether we fully realize it or not. We offer generous tax breaks to spur retirement savings

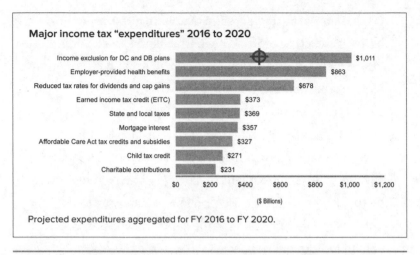

FIGURE 10.1 Flawed budget estimates lump savings deferrals in with true tax expenditures

Source: Congressional Joint Committee on Taxation, Estimates of Federal Tax Expenditures for Fiscal Years 2016-2020, January 2017.

because we want to enable American workers to grow their wages into wealth for the benefit of their families, for their own retirement security, and for the nation's economy as a whole.

As the chart in Figure 10.1 from Congress's Joint Committee on Taxation (JCT) shows, achieving these goals is not cheap—especially given the deeply flawed way Congress "scores" the "costs" of savings incentives. Allowing both defined benefit and defined contribution plans to defer taxes on the funds flowing into them will, by current scoring rules, "cost" the government over $1 trillion in forgone revenue—or tax "expenditures"—over the half-decade from 2016 to 2020. Multiple other tax expenditures—are also embedded in the code—for employer-provided healthcare, home ownership, charitable giving, and capital gains from investment risk-taking.

I leave it to others to debate whether these various tax deductions are appropriate, fair, and effective. But I must insist that retirement savings incentives are categorically different from other once-and-gone "expenditures." They are so different, in fact, that they should never have been lumped into this category to begin with. Unlike the other deductions on this chart, the taxes on retirement savings are not actually "forgiven." They are simply *postponed*—then taxed as ordinary income when workers begin to draw on their DB pensions or DC savings plans for income in retirement.

Most Americans contributing to workplace savings plans today choose to contribute pretax dollars because the contributions reduce their tax bills in an immediate and obvious way. In a standard 401(k), IRA, or similar investment structure, those contributions are exempted from a given year's income tax—and the savings can also grow tax free—but only until they are withdrawn. Again, those taxes are not forgiven—they are *deferred*. Unlike the once-and-gone tax breaks we grant for mortgage interest, employer-based healthcare, and other worthy causes, the taxes on most people's retirement savings will be paid as ordinary income—often many decades later, when workers use their savings to pay their expenses in retirement.

Of course, many workers today *can* voluntarily make "after-tax" contributions by choosing a Roth 401(k) or Roth IRA—which allows them to look forward to tax-free withdrawals on retirement. But relatively few eligible workers—so far—have chosen these options even where Roth-style accounts are available on the job.

Pension economists have debated for years whether pretax or post-tax retirement savings contribution better suits workers and/or tax collectors. Some believe that paying taxes up front is more advantageous for workers. Younger workers, they argue, have lower incomes and hence lower income tax rates. So they don't benefit very much from deductions because their effective income tax rates are usually less than 15 percent. Older workers, who may be paying 25 percent, 30 percent, or higher during their prime earning years, have far more to gain from pretax deductions. But they are also better positioned than young workers to afford higher savings. They are also old enough to appreciate the benefits of having tax-free "Roth" income once they do retire.

As to which option leaves more money with workers or with government, the only thing we can say is, "it depends." How old are the workers who are investing, and how long will they remain in the workforce? What is their tax bracket while working and in retirement? Will they keep earning income through their retirement years? What is the prevailing interest rate and stock market performance across the years of investment? How did their investment portfolios perform? How fast or slow will they convert these investments to cash?

The challenge of this calculation is wildly complex. But human nature is fairly clear on one point. Faced with a choice between taking the immediate gratification of a tax break *this year*—versus paying those taxes and then contributing to a life-long tax-free "Roth" account—fully 92 percent of workers take the immediate gratification of the current tax exemption. They simply don't worry about having to pay taxes on their savings decades later. The 8 percent of workers who voluntarily choose Roth options today may be taking the most beneficial financial path (again, it depends on their individual situation). But a split of 92 percent versus 8 percent in this binary choice suggests that the market has spoken clearly (as it so often does) regarding investor preference.

Tax Reform and Retirement Savings

Which brings us back to tax reform. While a broad tax reform would bring with it dozens, even hundreds of adjustments across our economy, when it comes to retirement, options for reform are few. These options are largely shaped, and, I would argue, *distorted*, by the way that Congress "scores" the cost to Treasury of offering any kind of retirement savings incentive.

Current scoring methodology, created by the Budget Act of 1974, requires congressional budget makers to "look out" 10 years—and no more—to calculate the cost to the Treasury of granting tax exemptions to retirement savers. So any increase in savings deferrals, whether caused by higher savings rates or more workers taking part in plans, will inevitably score as very costly over the first decade—even though those savings will be taxed, many years later, when savers draw them down to spend. By definition, this accounting convention is blind to the long term. But retirement assets rise, appreciate, and draw down over a half century or more.

Broadly speaking, there are three points in time or phases when taxation or tax exemption can impact retirement savings. Current income taxes can be imposed or exempted on wages saved in any given year—making them "pretax" or "after-tax" contributions. Taxes can also be either imposed or exempted on the interest, dividends, and capital gains earned in retirement accounts over the decades while these assets grow. Lastly, taxes can be levied or forgiven on funds that retirees draw from their accounts.

The earlier any worker contributes, the more time he or she will have to benefit from the miracle of compounding. Indeed, the sum of assets being taxed in withdrawal—after decades of compounding tax free—will most often be far greater than the worker's own lifetime of contributions. This makes long-term tax-free appreciation the most powerful benefit of either traditional pretax or Roth-style after-tax savings models.

The OECD Looks at EETs, TEEs, and All Points in Between

The Organization of Economic Cooperation and Development (OECD), in its *2016 Pensions Outlook*, surveyed the tax treatment of personal and workplace defined contribution retirement savings around the world and found a bewildering array of taxation schemes across the phases of savings—from initial contribution to the accumulation phase to withdrawal. Nations have adopted every variant of exemption and taxation—"E" or "T" at different stages of savings—that you can imagine.

A traditional American 401(k) or IRA can be conceived of as an exempt-exempt-taxed (EET) structure. EET, in fact, is the dominant model for most retirement savings in America. Tax exemptions are granted on both the initial contributions and any gains during accumulation—and then taxes are paid upon withdrawal. A Roth IRA or 401(k), by contrast, would be taxed-exempt-exempt (TEE).

We do, by the way, have other models in America. A standard bank account or a nonexempt brokerage account has a T-T-T structure that nets the most for the tax man. It's taxed all the way. But too few Americans know that we also have an E-E-E system—one that can earn the most for savers: It's called the Health Savings Account (HSA), and it is "triple-tax-free." Contributions are exempted, investment gains are exempt, and no tax is levied on withdrawals used to pay for healthcare expenses. It's Es all the way!

That's why many financial advisors suggest that workers first fund their workplace retirement savings plans up to the point of earning the full matching offer from employers, then rotate savings across to a "triple-tax-free" HSA account until they reach their legal limit and only then turn back to funding 401(k)s and IRAs—if, that is, they can still afford to save more.

But what is most interesting about the OECD's analysis of global retirement savings is that the designers of these global systems have studied very closely the example of the United States, which was an early innovator in defined contribution savings back in the 1980s.

When it comes to the goal of creating middle-class investment capital through capital markets, the pension economists of the OECD clearly "get it," and they are encouraging more nations to follow the U.S. example. They clearly see that it is in the long-term interest of any nation's retirement security, its fiscal health, and *its*

> *prospects for economic growth* to support workplace savings and capital market growth through the tax code.

For those of us in the retirement savings industry, it is frustrating to see politicians and interest groups pushing and pulling at our workplace retirement savings system in the context of tax reform. If we are to ever build the fully fleshed-out retirement system we've called Workplace Savings 4.0—to benefit virtually all workers—we need to clearly understand that our workplace savings incentives are "deferrals," not "expenditures." And we should all also know that the 10-year budgetary "window" that Congress uses to measure the "costs" of tax breaks for savings overstates their true cost by as much as 50 percent. All of us will pay taxes on our pretax DC savings once we draw them down.

It's true that any tax system that is fundamentally overhauled only once every 30 years is bound to have accumulated decades of unwarranted exemptions, narrow-cast tax breaks for industries, and a host of special-interest tweaks that build up like dead, dry tinder in an overgrown forest. We do need to clean the underbrush periodically—or risk fiscal forest fires down the road.

But as we aim for a tax code that (we hope) is more rational and transparent, the first principle for reform should be "Do no harm." The worst outcome of a poorly done tax reform would be to inadvertently lower Americans' already-too-low savings rates. Getting retirement tax policy right is not just about helping workers secure future incomes in retirement. It is the key to sustaining and building on America's comparative advantage over those nations that still have no well-funded base of mass investing for their working people.

The Broken Compass of Congressional "Scoring"

I have argued for years that Congress's use of a 10-year "window" to estimate the budget costs of retirement savings is not just dead wrong, but damaging—on multiple levels. It systematically overstates the "costs" of deferrals that flow back to the Treasury long after that 10-year "window" is closed. And it takes no account—zero, nada—of the huge benefits that these savings deliver to the government by reducing future dependency and fueling faster economic growth. It tempts policy makers to falsely pit national solvency against the personal solvency of American families. By doing so, it provides a perversely negative guide to policy choices. Virtually every serious policy maker in Congress agrees with me.

Yet changing budgetary "scoring" methodology that dates back to the 1970s seems as difficult as passing a major new act of legislation. We are likely, then, to go into our next major tax overhaul navigating by this broken compass. Sheer force of habit, inertia, and the debilitating spirit of "We've always done it this way" are just too strong.

Little wonder, then, that in early 2017, as talk of major tax reform heated up, new proposals emerged in some retirement policy circles in Washington to simply "step over" this scoring debate, perhaps even play a kind of jujitsu with the Budget Act's 10-year "window," by adopting either a hybrid of pretax traditional and post-tax Roth incentives—as Chairman Camp did—or by shifting fully to an "all-Roth" system.

By some estimates, going "full-Roth"—eliminating all pretax deferrals for future retirement savings—would "score" as much as $600 billion in 10-year "savings" for the Treasury. One variant of this proposal suggests that we could plough back $200 billion to $300 billion of these notional savings to pay for tax credits for retirement savers and also offer strong new financial incentives for companies that establish workplace plans. In theory, that could more than compensate individuals for lost deferrals and significantly increase overall coverage as more firms set plans up.

But there are more than a few risks. The first—and most serious—is that congressional tax reformers might simply "pocket" the alleged savings from switching to an "all-Roth" model, use that money only to reduce future deficits, and give no tax credits at all to savers who've lost their deferrals. Going "all-Roth" that way—without some very generous tax credits to make up for lost deferrals—would almost surely have a sharply negative impact on savings behavior. The shock might cause millions to cut back or even stop contributing to their plans.

Behavioral finance is clear that simplicity and automaticity work. And workers today have demonstrated their preference for traditional IRAs over Roth accounts because of their simplicity. Deductions are clearly expressed and calculated annually. Very few workers who could do so today actually choose a blend of traditional and Roth savings. But such a hybrid model may well be what emerges from this year's tax debates.

As I mentioned, many Washington tax experts expect the never-enacted "Camp Draft" of 2014 to serve as a guide for the next generation of tax reforms. The Camp proposal would have set corporate income tax rates at 25 percent and created tax brackets of 25 percent and 35 percent for nearly all workers. It would have repealed the unloved and outdated Alternative

Minimum Tax and opted for a cross-border territorial tax system that has long been advocated by business leaders and economists.

To partially pay for these changes, Camp proposed a kind of "half-Rothification." His bill would have allowed retirement savers to still contribute some money to a traditional IRA and get a deferral. But beyond a specified limit, any further contributions would have to be after-tax money and go into Roth accounts.

The Camp draft was a down-the-middle kind of tax reform. Its carefully crafted compromises sought to give and take something from all stakeholders—taxpayers and tax collectors alike. It sought revenue neutrality (more or less, given that no one can predict the future) and aimed at "distributional neutrality"— meaning that changes would not weigh too heavily on any single income cohort.

If Congress opts for a "Camp 2.0" approach, we will have much to debate in terms of the fiscal implications of this plan for the government and the savings implications for American families. But from the perspective of a finance practitioner, a modified "Camp" approach might very well increase the complexity of retirement savings and take us in precisely the wrong direction.

Any proposal that mandates a blend of traditional and Roth options would require workplace savers to annually revisit their investment mix. What proportion of savings should be deployed to traditional accounts and what proportion to Roth? And how should this calculation change over time, factoring in new circumstances and liabilities?

With no clear actuarial signals as to the long-term benefit of either savings format (each worker would be uniquely impacted), workers would find themselves where they were decades ago, before automatic enrollment and automatic allocation, when they were forced to choose from among dozens of investment allocations and hope for the best.

Given that most Americans today choose traditional pretax savings deferrals, might a mandatory conversion to Roth result in reduced levels of savings? That's a tough question—with no clear answers.

Many analysts presume that those who wish to save *will save* and that the impact of introducing more Roth options will be negligible. Academic studies of savers' behavior in plans that have added Roth options to more traditional tax-deferred savings plans find little change—up or down.

We do know that a partial or complete conversion to Roth would have different impacts on different kinds of savers. And if this overhaul were to happen *without* a generous package of countervailing tax credits, then younger and lower-income workers might well be discouraged once they noticed their cost of setting aside savings rising paycheck to paycheck.

The departure of lower-income workers could negatively affect employers, too, by shifting their workplace plans toward noncompliance with "nondiscrimination" rules mandated by the Employee Retirement Income Security Act (ERISA). These rules aim to ensure that workers at all income levels take part in workplace plans so that their benefits are not concentrated solely among highly compensated employees and executives.

With so many variables in play, it is exceedingly difficult to forecast what a shift to an "all-Roth" structure would do to Americans' savings behavior. But we do know that complexity breeds uncertainty, leading too often to glorified guesswork.

Introducing new complexity, forcing workers to guesstimate the impact of these choices over the course of decades of work, taxes, and retirement, would create new minefields of error and risk. Behavioral experts are quite clear on how workers respond to opaque risk; they shut down. So increasing complexity in our retirement savings could simply lead to reduced savings across the board.

If Congress were to decide on a mandatory shift away from traditional savings deferral, then the "simplicity doctrine" would suggest that rather than adopting a complex "hybrid" system we simply bite the bullet and make a once-and-done, permanent shift to the all-Roth model.

Such a clean break to an all-Roth model for future savings (while "grandfathering" existing investments) would be a shock, at least initially. But it would also be simpler in terms of accounting, employee education, investment strategies, and income projection. It might even help close our huge "coverage gap" and bring millions more workers into savings plans— provided this major change included generous tax credits to companies that set up plans and to individual savers who would be losing their familiar tax deferrals.

In the spirit of colonial New England, then, let me suggest one principle that should guide this type of retirement tax reform: *"No Rothification without tax-creditization!"*

Now, I don't think we'll ever see a crowd of demonstrators carrying that sign. But I'd support them if I did. Because I believe that any consideration of shifting to an all-Roth model for retirement savings won't work well unless it includes a full array of new—and permanent—savings incentives to ease the transition:

- Robust tax credits for small employers to establish new plans with auto-enrollment and a specified minimum deferral
- Simplification of retirement plan regulations to facilitate employer participation and to make it easier for workers to do the right thing
- Expansion of the Savers Credit to attract lower-income employees into plans, together with expanded eligibility that would make it available to fully half of all taxpayers
- Expansion of contribution limits by up to one-third so that senior managers and small business owners could increase their overall deferrals
- Creation of a Universal Roth IRA for short-term and long-term family needs and a Starter 401(k), with streamlined regulation, for small businesses
- Creation of a Children's Savings Account to pay for education and to help young adults with financial flexibility after college
- Adjustment or elimination of the required minimum distribution rules (RMDs) so that workers can stay in the workforce while also protecting their accumulated assets
- Establishment of Multiple Employer Plans (MEPs) through which unaffiliated small businesses could create pooled 401(k) plans that take advantage of economies of scale and their aggregated pricing power

"Rothification" of the American workplace retirement system would be a major change. But it need not be traumatic if the loss of deferrals is fully compensated by strong financial incentives for individual workers to save and for companies to offer savings plans. Taken together, the tax incentives mentioned above might generate as much as $1 trillion in new retirement savings over a decade and increase middle-class family retirement income substantially. Such a reform could also focus most tax credits on workers making less than $100,000 per year—thereby making the whole system more equitable. But "Rothifying" our savings system without such offsets could be very damaging.

That's why my message to retirement policy makers is simple: don't hurry, don't presume. Keep your eye on the prize of higher overall savings rates. Proceed with caution. When it comes to impacting retirement savings, tax reform needs a scalpel, not a meat cleaver. An awful lot is at stake—and at risk.

Remember that our existing laws have fostered a multitrillion-dollar pool of retirement savings, owned by tens of millions of workers and channeled through the world's richest capital markets. Build on that. Tax reformers should aim to realize our workplace savings system's full potential—by raising workers' saving rates, offering plans to all, and bringing millions more workers aboard the savings train.

By contrast, any new legislation that inadvertently reduces savings could erode the vast flows of patient capital that American workers channel into our capital markets with every paycheck. These savings drive economic growth, which in turn generates higher future tax receipts that can bring down government deficits over the long run. Strong, sustainable economic growth is by far the least painful, and the most *American*, way to meet our long-term fiscal challenges.

Our workplace savings plans are proven engines of such growth.

As this book goes to print, no one knows whether Congress will actually be able to enact a comprehensive reform of the tax code—or how that may affect retirement savings. But even as Congress wrestles with that challenge, I urge our leaders in Washington to focus on the larger, long-term questions at stake:

- Do the proposed changes help or hurt Americans' ability to save for our future?
- Does any given change free up "scorable" resources that can be used to increase contributions, expand coverage, and foster the creation of new savings plans?
- Will the changes expand the overall market for retirement savings by increasing flows into retirement accounts and bringing more workers into the system?
- How much additional revenue might the government generate, and how much additional savings might workers accumulate down the road—not just in the 10-year budgetary scoring "window", but over half a century or more?

Our retirement finance mission is measured in generations. The tax code meant to advance this mission should be fair, transparent, and supportive of American workers for generations into the future.

Let our leaders hear from you that Americans' savings are not playthings for politicians to manipulate. These assets are the American people's hard-earned wealth, the seed corn of our economy's future. All of us—from Wall Street to Main Street, from mom and pop to the U.S. Congress and Treasury, should be pulling in the same direction—to help more Americans benefit from a retirement savings system that has achieved so much, and can still become so much better.

We really are all in this together.

THE PATH TO AMERICAN RENEWAL

I've said it before and I'll say it again—
America's best days are yet to come.
—RONALD REAGAN

I believe that the continued expansion of mass investing through workplace savings plans is the single best way to give all Americans a stake in a growing economy. And I believe that this kind of inclusion is essential if we want to forge a broad consensus for policy action aimed at restoring the 3-percent-plus economic growth this country achieved during most of my lifetime.

Many Americans today doubt the ability of politicians, government, and our financial markets to secure their future. This is understandable given that the deep market crisis of 2008–2009 hammered home values and 401(k) balances alike. Perhaps more importantly, but more difficult to measure, the crisis damaged Americans' sense of stability, fair play, and trust in our institutions.

In the years since the crisis, our financial markets have delivered robust returns and home prices have recovered—especially in select zip codes. Yet, there is no getting around the fact that the recovery has benefited some individuals and regions far more than others. Wages have decoupled from financial returns, and we are still struggling with middle-class income stagnation that has been with us for a generation.

America's economic growth rate has been falling for decades, from 4.5 percent a year in the 1960s, to 3.5 percent in the 1980s, to less than 2 percent a year since the turn of the century. As with returns on investment or interest paid on bank deposits, economic growth compounds. A difference of 1 percent up or down can make a huge difference over the course of a lifetime—and not just in economic terms, but politically, socially, and psychologically.

Our long, unpleasant bout of slow growth and stagnant incomes has fueled an ugly, rancorous political environment in America and led many to believe that we have become a zero-sum society in which anyone's gain is someone else's loss. That's the strange political fruit of what former Treasury Secretary Larry Summers calls "secular stagnation."

For decades after World War II, robust economic growth made it easy for the United States to integrate women, minorities, and other groups into the workforce, and to take in millions of immigrants. But for the past 20+ years, sluggish growth has given our public discourse an embittered tone, with many seeking scapegoats for economic dislocation—illegal immigrants, overseas trading partners, "coastal elites," or simply "the one percent."

This subpar growth has dampened Americans' can-do spirit and spilled over into raw-toned populist politics. As has happened in many other nations, a deep recession's impact on growth makes everything worse: household balance sheets, business expansion, government deficits, and national morale. Along the way, we've lost the sense of bipartisan cooperation and compromise that once prevailed on incentives for growth, international trade, immigration, and entitlement reform.

It is my hope that our political leaders at the federal and local levels will soon find a way to transcend partisan politics and find common ground. Whatever our party affiliation, we need to reboot America's spirit and come together across party lines to deal with the big-picture issues of national infrastructure, energy, science and medical research, education, and promotion of U.S. manufacturing.

These are the kinds of massive long-term investments that can generate a road map for our economy and lift Americans' standards of living for decades into the future. And I very much want all Americans to benefit from them, not only as workers but also as investors and owners.

Let's remind ourselves what it means to be an American. We are the country that invested in big ideas in one industry after another—transportation, telecommunications, aviation and aerospace, information technology, medicine and biotech, the Internet, and mobile computing. We are the nation that taught the rest of the world to dream big. We inspired millions to want to invest in America, get an education in America, come to live here, and become American citizens themselves.

I believe that if we bring the tens of millions of American workers with no retirement savings into workplace plans— including those who work in small businesses, at lower wages, or in the "gig economy" as contract labor, we will give them a real stake in free enterprise and economic growth. At the same time, we can also advance social justice by helping millions of Americans who have literally no financial assets today plant the seeds of future wealth.

But the most important gains from tackling the retirement challenge would be psychological, political, and cultural. By demonstrating that we can take on a huge and complex challenge—and showing that a government of the people can actually benefit all the people—we would rekindle the American spirit that has inspired hardworking, self-reliant people all over the world for the past 250 years.

That's a goal worth fighting for.

I hope you will join me.

SEVEN EASY STEPS TO RETIREMENT SECURITY (AND WHY IT MATTERS)

I trust this whole book has made clear my passion for comprehensively solving America's retirement savings challenge. And I am convinced we have the insights and resources to do just that. But much of what I've advocated depends on action by Congress and federal regulators. And we simply can't be sure they will act—or when—so here's seven ways *you* can act right now to get from here to security.

1. **Insure yourself and your family for life, health, and disability.** You can do this either through a plan at work or as an individual. Without basic insurance coverage, anything else you save could be wiped out—instantly—by death, serious medical costs, or a disabling illness or accident. You should cover this base no matter what.

2. **Build an emergency savings fund of at least three to six months of expenses.** You never know when you may need it. Having it gives you much more maneuvering room. Money is liquid freedom. Have some ready, just in case.

3. **Minimize debt.** Avoid any high-interest debt like the plague. Pay off your credit card balances every month in full. The only routine debts you should have are for investment in your own "human capital" like student loans or for equipment and capital expenditures to set up your own business, or for a mortgage to buy a home.

4. **Buy a home when you can afford to, and don't buy more home than you can afford.** The deductibility of mortgage interest is one of the best (and most politically secure) tax breaks available today. Any mortgage is, in effect, a form of forced savings you impose on yourself. And the buildup of home equity plus savings on rent become for most people a major share of lifelong wealth. Your home isn't just your castle; it's likely to become your biggest asset.

5. **Maximize savings in workplace tax-deferred plans or, if you are self-employed, set up an IRA.** In either case, aim to save the maximum allowed by law. If your company offers a savings match, then put aside enough money to capture that match in full. Employer "matches" are the closest thing you'll ever see to free money; don't leave them on the table. Also, aim to get to a savings rate of 10 percent or more in your workplace plan as soon as you can afford to. Make that a lifelong habit. You'll have no regrets. And if your employer offers a Health Savings Account (HSA), by all means take full advantage of it. *HSAs are triple-tax-free.* This means you pay no taxes on money you save, on gains

on investments over time, or even on withdrawals, provided they are for medical expenses. Triple-tax protection is uniquely valuable. Even the healthiest people will have doctor's bills to pay at some point.

6. **Diversify your investments** broadly across the stock and bond markets, with high exposure (75 to 80 percent) to stocks in your twenties and thirties, shifting to a more conservative mix (say 70 percent bonds and 30 percent equities) as your retirement date nears. A simple way to do this is to choose a single target date fund close to the time you plan to retire and put most of your savings into it. Note: target date funds typically have broad diversification across hundreds of individual stocks and bonds; they shift your allocation and reduce your risk—automatically—over time without your having to make any specific investment calls.

7. **Secure at least some guaranteed lifetime income.** Consider investing in annuities or guaranteed drawdown funds by your late forties or early fifties. These are already available in some workplace plans today. There will be many more as Workplace Savings 4.0 models evolve. These products can protect you from the worst risk most people fear about retirement: outliving their money. Longevity risk is real; provide for it.

8. **Most important of all: enjoy yourself.** If you do your best to follow the seven steps outlined above, you will be on track to retirement security. Knowing that, I hope, should give you peace of mind to enjoy America's oldest promise: the chance to pursue happiness through life, love, family, and a rewarding career. Life is precious. Make each day of it count. Isn't that the whole point of saving in the first place?

HOW TO FIX SOCIAL SECURITY

What follows is a thoroughly bipartisan op-ed piece jointly negotiated and drafted with my friend and business community colleague James Roosevelt Jr. in 2012. At the time, Jim was the CEO of Tufts Health Plan, one of Boston's leading healthcare providers; he had also served a term as associate commissioner for retirement policy of the Social Security Administration. He happens, incidentally, to be the grandson of Social Security's great champion, President Franklin Delano Roosevelt, whose values he shares.

It took us a fair amount of back-and-forth bargaining to agree on a set of reforms to bring Social Security to solvency for the twenty-first century. The changes we agreed on were almost exactly balanced between new revenues and reductions in future benefits' growth. We both had to make concessions we didn't like. But finding common ground to preserve and secure Social Security itself was easy; since we both saw it as vital for all working Americans, we bargained for a solution in good faith. Of course, neither Jim nor I were running for public office, which made it much easier for us to arrive at a solution.

When real politicians sit down to work out a compromise to make this vital system solvent for the twenty-first century, they are going to need all the support that we, the people, can give them as citizens.

May 9, 2012—The *Boston Globe* Editorial Page

How to Fix Social Security

By James Roosevelt Jr. and Robert L. Reynolds

A recent report by the Social Security Board of Trustees that the system's trust funds could be exhausted by 2033—three years earlier than the prior year's estimate—ought to be a wake-up call for Democrats and Republicans to put country above party. It's time to stop kicking the can down the road and work together toward a goal we all share: retirement security. As Americans live longer and our population ages, we need a reliable retirement system with strong public and private elements.

We are two executives with different views—one an FDR Democrat who heads a nonprofit health plan, the other a Reagan Republican who leads a private investment firm. But on the core issue of retirement security, we share common ground. We believe that Social Security, the most successful government program in our country's history, is an indispensable base for all Americans' retirement security. It needs to be preserved, and its solvency guaranteed. In addition, the system should be backed up by a robust private workplace savings system that all working Americans have access to.

Social Security does have assets to meet its current obligations. It holds $2.7 trillion in special federal government bonds in its trust fund. But as its trustees' reports show, the system also faces a multitrillion dollar funding shortfall over the next 75 years. Absent reform, trust fund assets could be exhausted by 2033—leading to an abrupt drop of roughly 25 percent in a current 40-year-old's future benefits. The uncertainty that this funding gap creates is what undermines so many peoples' confidence in the system today.

The good news is that relatively manageable reforms today can make the system solvent for generations— and avoid the vastly more painful cuts that continued delay would cause. There is certainly plenty of precedent for action.

Congress has enacted 10 significant Social Security bills over the years. Each brought the program back into balance under changing economic and demographic circumstances. The most recent of these reforms came in 1983 when President Ronald Reagan and House Speaker Thomas "Tip" O'Neill crafted a bipartisan package of revenue increases and benefit reductions that put Social Security on firm ground for a full generation. We need just such a balanced approach now, reflecting new economic and demographic realities—especially rising longevity.

On the revenue side, we should hold tax rates steady, but gradually phase in a rise in the current $110,100 ceiling on wages subject to Social Security contributions. Until the 1990s, that ceiling reached roughly 90 percent of all wages. We should move back up to that 90 percent level by 2020 and then index the ceiling to future wage gains. This reflects the income gains that the most successful Americans have seen in the past generation. Lifting the FICA ceiling would be far preferable to the "means testing" that some have proposed—which would deny benefits to the more affluent. We could also enhance revenues by requiring all future state and local government employees to join the Social Security system, a reform that would also, over time, make local pension costs more manageable.

On the benefits side, we should change the way we calculate the cost-of-living adjustment for all beneficiaries, by utilizing a revised Consumer Price Index which most economists agree more accurately reflects the rate of inflation for the expenses most seniors incur. Such a change would curb the rate of increase in benefits for future generations of retirees, but no one would actually get less money. This change in the benefits formula should be structured so that it makes future economic growth a clear positive—enabling incoming revenues to grow somewhat faster than promised benefits so that the system becomes truly self-sustaining.

Lastly, we should accelerate the rise in Social Security's full-benefit retirement age from age 67 to 68 by 2030 and then index the full-benefit age for future generations to gains in longevity. Life expectancy past age 65 has risen nearly 50 percent since 1940, when Social Security first began regular monthly payments.

That said, we should improve disability options for those engaged in physically demanding jobs. No one expects coal miners or telephone line crews to work into their late 60s.

Based on estimates included in the 2010 report of the Social Security system's expert advisory board, these proposals could eliminate nearly all of Social Security's funding shortfall over the next 75 years.

We should then back up a solvent Social Security system with as close to universal access to workplace-based private savings as possible. This requires preserving all existing tax deferrals for savings through 401(k)s, IRAs, and other retirement vehicles, and then extending coverage to all working Americans by adopting a great, bipartisan idea—the payroll-deduction Automatic IRA. These tax deferrals are not part of America's deficit problem. In fact, the savings they foster are key to funding economic growth and robust capital markets. Savings-led growth is the best long-term solution for our deficits.

Creating a truly reliable public-private retirement system would do far more than just help restore Americans' confidence in their personal futures. It would boost market confidence worldwide. It might also revive the American people's belief that our two political parties can look past their differences—as we have—to find common ground for the country we love. Rebooting that shared faith might just be the greatest benefit of all.

"DEAR 45" LETTER FOR THE U.S. CHAMBER OF COMMERCE

During the 2016 presidential campaign, the U.S. Chamber of Commerce sponsored a series of "Dear 45" letters to the next president from business leaders across a wide variety of industries. These letters ran in newspapers, magazines, and other media across the country during the campaign. I was honored to be asked to write on the subject of solving America's retirement savings challenge—which, as you will see, I view as an opportunity, not a "crisis."

To the 45th President of the United States

From: Bob Reynolds

Dear 45,

From the moment you lift your hand from the Bible at your inauguration, the American people will look to you for leadership to restore their shaken faith that our government can truly work "for the people."

One of the most promising ways to do that would be taking on—and solving—America's retirement security challenge. Working Americans routinely cite concern about their retirement futures as their single greatest worry. The good news is that as our new president you can meet this challenge on a bipartisan basis and help spur stronger economic growth in the process.

Having spent over three decades building up America's workplace savings system, I can assure you that the pathway to meeting this nation's retirement challenge is clear. The challenges are not intellectual—they are political. That is why we need your leadership.

The first step is to work with Congress to make Social Security solvent for the long term. To be politically feasible, this reform must include both benefit adjustments and enhanced revenues and it must not hurt low-to-moderate income workers.

This grand bargain can only happen if our new president takes it on—with passion, vision, and flexibility. Action is urgent. You will have a brief "window" to act on this challenge and delay will only make solutions tougher and more painful.

Social Security solvency should be matched by a drive to strengthen and expand the private workplace savings system. This system—401(k) plans and the like—is already enabling tens of millions of workers to save for their retirement futures. But this great success story does need strengthening.

The best path to positive change would be to focus on what is already working well in today's workplace savings plans—and extend their coverage to all. It will be possible to work with Congress to find ways to extend workplace savings coverage to all. The goal should be securing access to on-the-job savings for every American who pays Social Security tax. Closing this "coverage gap" will put millions more workers on track to security.

You should also work to spread the best practices seen in today's successful retirement plans to every workplace plan in America. Experience shows us—beyond doubt—that plan designs that automatically enroll all workers and raise their savings to 10% or more get the job done. Such plans are already helping tens of millions of workers today to move towards the system's ultimate goal: secure incomes for life. Because they are automatic, such plan designs make success *easy*—and failure *hard*. And proven success should become America's retirement savings model.

These basic changes—a solvent Social Security system plus universal access to well-designed workplace savings plans—would dramatically improve all Americans' retirement security. Imagine the positive impact on Americans' faith in their government—and in themselves. And there would be other incredibly valuable benefits, too.

By directing the retirement savings of millions more citizens into America's capital markets, we would assure all working Americans a real stake in our free enterprise system. Workers themselves, one paycheck at a time, would provide the patient, long-term capital needed to support more entrepreneurship, more job creation, and more rapid economic growth. Personal solvency would strengthen national solvency.

So don't think of retirement policy as only a "challenge." Think of it as a great opportunity.

With your leadership, we can transform a source of worry into an engine of American prosperity—and renewed national pride.

Sincerely,

Robert L. Reynolds
President and CEO, Great-West Financial and
Putnam Investments

GLOSSARY

Annuities, Annuitization—Annuities are income contracts purchased from financial institutions. Typically used to provide guaranteed income in retirement, these contracts may be purchased before investors retire, upon retirement, or at some time later during retirement. The period between purchase and payout is called the accumulation phase; the period in which the contract pays investors is called the annuitization phase.

Automaticity—The creation of default options, most typically the automatic placement of workers into savings plans and into investment strategies that aim to benefit their long-term prospects for financial security in retirement. Examples include auto-enrollment, auto allocation, auto-escalation of deferrals, and automatic engagement of guaranteed income solutions in retirement. The full suite of automatic choices is sometimes termed "full auto."

Auto-IRA—Principle by which workers may be automatically enrolled into Individual Retirement Accounts (IRAs) in the workplace. Currently being rolled out in several states for workers without access to private workplace defined contribution savings plans.

Behavioral Economics/Behavioral Finance—the application of psychological and sociological principles as a means of analyzing financial decision making and behaviors such as savings plan enrollment, asset allocation, risk engagement, and risk tolerance.

Birthright Retirement Accounts—This concept would have the federal government establish a small savings account for every newborn child in America, effectively creating a lifelong investment glide path for retirement.

Choice Architecture—A behavioral finance principle in which savings and investment options are presented in a manner designed to guide workers to optimal choices. Examples include automatic enrollment, opt-outs, and automatic allocation to risk-managed investments.

Contingent Labor—Workers other than full-time employees, employed as contractors, consultants, freelancers, or temporary contract workers. These workers pay both employer and employee portions of Social Security payroll taxes and do not participate in employer-sponsored workplace savings plans. These workers are often described as participating in the "gig economy."

Coverage Gap—The persistent shortfall of worker coverage by workplace retirement savings plans. Many small employers cannot afford to administer ERISA-compliant workplace savings plans. As many as half of American workers fall into this gap.

Deferred Income Annuities (Longevity Annuities)—Also known as DIAs, these are income contracts between investors and insurance companies in which investors purchase the annuity on a given date and then begin collecting guaranteed lifetime income beginning years or decades later. DIAs allow retirees to keep more assets in risky markets like stocks because the pending DIA effectively mitigates overall portfolio risk.

Defined Benefit Plans (pension plans)—Pension plans in which benefits are determined by length of service and salary. Pension fund trustees own and invest assets, providing promised benefits that terminate upon death.

Defined Contribution Plans—workplace savings plans for retirement, education, and healthcare defined by volume of income deferred and invested, rather than by level of benefits earned by pension fund membership. Accumulated assets are owned and invested by workers and may be passed on to heirs.

- 401(k)—Workplace savings plans at private companies
- 403(b) plan—Workplace savings plans at public sector organizations

- 529 plan—College savings plans
- Health Savings Accounts (HSAs)—Triple-tax-incented savings plans for high deductible health insurance plans

Dependency Ratio (Support Ratio)—Economists contrast the number of workers currently in the labor force with those out of the labor force (retirees) and use this ratio to gauge the sustainability of retirement finance architecture. When traditional pensions were established generations ago, there were many workers for each retiree; today this ratio is aggressively narrowing, drawing into question the sustainability of the retirement finance architecture. For example, in 1950 the U.S. support ratio was 16:1; today it is 3:1, and in 2035 it will be 2:1.

Employment Retirement Income Security Act of 1974 (ERISA)—This federal law established minimum standards for private pensions and provided federal income tax rules associated with employee benefit plans. ERISA obliged plans sponsors to disclose information to beneficiaries, established standards and practices for plan fiduciaries, designated regulatory responsibilities for the federal Departments of Labor and Treasury and the Pension Benefit Guaranty Corporation (PBGC), and provided for legal remedy in the federal courts.

Financial Literacy—A basic understanding of personal finance topics including retirement finance, investment, insurance, educational finance, tax planning, etc. Observing that many individuals persist in making suboptimal financial choices, many industry experts have concluded that consumers would be better served by behavioral finance principles that guide them to more optimal decision making and planning rather than by expensive educational programs that have limited impact.

Income Replacement Ratio—Retirement income divided by working income. Used as a measure of the adequacy of annuitized retirement savings.

Individual Retirement Account (IRA)—IRAs are tax-advantaged retirement investment accounts typically invested in target date funds, mutual funds, or other securities. Unlike 401(k)s, which are accounts sponsored by employers, IRAs are standalone accounts that individuals open on their own.

Lifetime Income Score (LIS)—This research, undertaken by Empower Retirement and Brightwork Partners, takes into account all sources of future retiree financial benefits—Social Security, traditional pensions, defined contribution workplace savings plans such as 401(k)s, savings, insurance, home equity, and shares in business ownership. LIS surveys calculate replacement percentages of preretirement income, noting the positive impacts of access to workplace savings plans, automatic enrollment, automatic savings escalation, and work with financial advisors.

Longevity Risk—Any financial risk related to increasing life expectancy. Insurance companies calculate whether their policies can profitably stand behind their guarantees. Pension funds must calculate whether they have sufficient funds to comply with benefits promised to their pensioners. Individual retirement savers must calculate whether they have accumulated sufficient financial assets, together with their Social Security benefits, to provide for themselves in retirement. As global longevity increases, all of these systems are strained worldwide.

Modern Portfolio Theory (MPT)—A foundational predicate of modern pension fund investing, MPT helps investors to optimize the returns that they can expect from a given level of risk. MPT established that returns and risk are inherently linked. This in turn allowed organizations and individuals to calibrate their desire for returns with their risk tolerance.

Multiple Employer Plans (MEPs)—MEPs are workplace savings plans sponsored by groups of employers, rather than single employers. MEPs promise economies of scale and efficiencies that can drive down the administrative burdens and cost of workplace savings plans. MEPs have traditionally been limited to related groups of employers (such as industry associations).

Many retirement policy experts are calling for the establishment of "open MEPs" that would dramatically increase their usage, offering sustainable workplace savings plans to workers at small employers that cannot independently afford to establish ERISA-compliant plans such as 401(k)s.

Nudge Economics—In behavioral economics, a nudge is a kind of positive reinforcement that can be engineered to urge individuals or groups to make decisions. Typically seen as an efficient alternative to regulations, mandates, and enforcement, a nudge offers incentives such as tax credits and regulatory relief to individuals or groups. In retirement savings, nudges like automatic enrollment, deferral, and allocation have resulted in dramatically improved financial results as compared with purely voluntary offerings.

Pay-as-You-Go Plans (PAYGO)—Generally speaking, private company pensions and U.S. state-government employee pensions are supported by an investment fund that finances pension payouts. Many traditional public-sector pension funds are unfunded. For example, U.S. government defined benefit pensions are paid out of current tax receipts. Many government pensions around the world are also pay-as-you-go.

Pension Protection Act of 2006 (PPA)—The PPA capped 20 years of retirement policy evolution by endorsing a series of best practices in workplace savings plans that had been inspired by behavioral finance research and experiments by a handful of progressive plan sponsors. The PPA, in effect, marked the first time that Congress and top policy makers recognized defined contribution plans as the primary source of future retirement income and acted to treat these plans as a system.

Qualified Default Investment Options (QDIAs)—The Pension Protection Act of 2006 established legal safe harbor for ERISA-compliant workplace savings plans that undertook auto-enrollment into "qualified" stable value funds, balanced funds, target date funds, and managed accounts.

Retirement Readiness—This term describes a holistic preparation for retirement that includes retirement savings, Social Security, healthcare insurance, Medicare, housing, and other factors. Investors and their advisors should factor in their entire financial circumstance—assets, benefits, and liabilities—in assessing retirement readiness.

Revenue Act of 1978—This rather humble legislation was primarily dedicated to routine administrative elements like widening tax brackets and reducing the number of tax rates in the U.S. Internal Revenue code. But the law also added a section 401(k) to the Internal Revenue Code that reinvented America's multitrillion-dollar retirement finance system by launching the defined contribution workplace savings revolution.

Section 401(k)—A provision of the Revenue Act of 1978 that was intended to allow companies to offer pretax savings plans as supplements to traditional pensions—but opened the way to the creation of today's multitrillion-dollar 401(k) industry, which has become the primary source for most working Americans' future retirement income.

Sequence-of-Returns Risk—Retirement savings investors must be concerned with a little-known and potentially dangerous risk regarding the "sequence of returns"—meaning outsized gains or huge losses—in financial markets in the years just after retirement.

Target Date Funds (TDFs)—These investment funds, typically used by retirement and education savers, are built around an investment algorithm that evolves investment exposures along a "glide path." Funds engage high-return, high-risk equities early in the investment period, gradually shifting exposure toward lower-risk fixed-income securities as target dates approach.

Workplace Savings 1.0—The initial surge of defined contribution savings plan adoption beginning in the early 1980s as many companies converted to 401(k)-style payroll deduction plans. This period was marked by purely voluntary enrollment, steadily expanding investment options, and a risk shift from companies to individuals. This raised the number of DC savers past the number of DB plan participants by about 1985.

Workplace Savings 2.0—From the early 1990s to 2006, this period saw the emergence of target date funds and their embedded advice and "glide paths" as a prime choice for plan defaults. It also saw early experiments with auto-enrollment and savings escalation.

Workplace Savings 3.0—The Pension Protection Act of 2006 launched a qualitatively new phase in workplace savings by endorsing automatic plan design as valid and guiding plan participants to improved default choices of target date and balanced funds that offer much improved chances of attaining retirement readiness. PPA also offers strong legal "safe harbor" protection to plan sponsors who adopt these design features. We are yet to fully implement such automatic designs across all existing workplace savings plans.

Workplace Savings 4.0—This is a next generation series of improvements to workplace plans that is already emerging in the marketplace as progressive plan sponsors introduce lifetime income options into plans along with healthcare cost and peer comparison tools to spur higher savings. A new industry norm of 10-percent-plus savings deferrals is also emerging. But realizing the full potential of Empower Retirement's Workplace Savings 4.0 vision will require new legislation, wise regulatory support, and even stronger safe harbors. The reforms proposed in the 4.0 model would, if adopted, substantially solve America's retirement savings challenge.

BIBLIOGRAPHY

The academic, industry, and journalistic library on American retirement policy is immense, as you'll see from the full Bibliography that follows. But for those who simply want to gain key insights into the themes that have shaped *From Here to Security*, the following books have made a particularly powerful impact with insights into retirement finance.

Automatic: Changing the Way America Saves, by William G. Gale, J. Mark Iwry, David C. John, and Lina Walker. Lays out a valuable template for Auto-IRAs—accounts that may be a critical element in resolving the coverage gap.

Falling Short: The Coming Retirement Crisis and What to Do About It, by Alicia H. Munnell, Charles D. Ellis, and Andrew D. Eschtruth. A concise and comprehensive overview of America's retirement coverage gap.

Nudge: Improving Decisions About Health, Wealth and Happiness, by Richard H. Thaler and Cass R. Sunstein. Introduced the world to behavioral economics and presents valuable behavioral alternatives to punitive regulation and expensive enforcement.

The Ownership Society: How the Defined Contribution Paradigm Changed America, by Edward A. Zelinsky. Solid overview of the defined contribution savings system and how it changed American retirement finance.

The People's Pension: The Struggle to Defend Social Security Since Reagan, by Eric Laursen. A monumental contemporary history of Social Security—America's universal defined benefit pension plan.

Save More Tomorrow: Practical Behavioral Finance Solutions to Improve 401(k) Plans, by Shlomo Benartzi. Articulates the valuable impact of escalation into automatic retirement savings plan enrollment.

U.S. Pension Reform: Lessons from Other Countries, by Martin Neil Baily and Jacob Funk Kirkegaard. Offers valuable comparative analysis between U.S. and overseas retirement finance systems and makes clear that the U.S. combination of Social Security and private pension savings is unique.

FULL BIBLIOGRAPHY

Adams, Nevin, and Jack Vanderhei, 2012. "Ready or Not: The Impact of Retirement-Plan Design." *Milken Institute Review.*

Aegon, 2016. *A Retirement Wake-Up Call: The Aegon Retirement Readiness Survey.* Aegon Center for Longevity and Retirement.

Agnew, Julie, 2013. *Australia's Retirement System: Strengths, Weaknesses and Reforms.* Boston College Center for Retirement Research.

Antunes, Pedro, Alicia Macdonald, and Matthew Stewart. *Boosting Retirement Readiness and the Economy Through Financial Advice.* Ottawa: The Conference Board of Canada, 2014.

Austin, Rob, 2013. "The Impact of Behavioral Economics on Retirement Plans." *Benefits Quarterly.*

Australian Centre for Financial Studies, 2016. *Melbourne Mercer Global Pension Index.*

Baily, Martin Neil, and Jacob Funk Kirkegaard, 2009. *U.S. Pension Reform: Lessons from Other Countries.* Washington, DC: Peterson Institute for International Economics.

Belbase, Anek, Alicia H. Munnell, Nari Rhee, and Geoffrey T. Sanzenbacher, 2016. *State Savings Initiatives: Lessons from California and Connecticut.* Boston College Center for Retirement Research.

Benartzi, Shlomo, and Roger Lewin, 2015. *Thinking Smarter: Seven Steps to Fulfilling Retirement and Life.* New York, NY: Portfolio-Penguin.

Benartzi, Shlomo, and Roger Lewin, 2012. *Save More Tomorrow: Practical Behavioral Finance Solutions to Improve 401(k) Plans.* New York, NY: Allianz Global Investors, Center for Behavioral Finance.

Benartzi, Shlomo, and Robert Thaler, 2001. "Naïve Diversification Strategies in Retirement Savings Plans," *American Economic Review.*

Beshears, John, James Choi, David Laibson, Brigitte Madrian, and Brian Weller, 2008. *Public Policy and Saving for Retirement: The Autosave Features of the Pension Protection Act of 2006.* National Bureau of Economic Research.

Biggs, Andrew G., 2014. *Retirement Savings 2.0: Updating Savings Policy for the Modern Economy.* American Enterprise Institute.

Biggs, Andrew G., and Sylvester J. Schieber, 2015. *Why Americans Don't Face a Retirement Crisis.* American Enterprise Institute.

Biggs, Andrew G., and Sylvester J. Schieber, 2014. *Is There a Retirement Crisis?* National Affairs.

Bipartisan Policy Center, 2016. *Securing Our Financial Future: Report of the Commission on Retirement Security and Personal Savings.* Washington DC: Bipartisan Policy Center.

BNY Mellon, 2016. *The DC Plan of the Future: DB Principles for the DC Generation.* New York: Bank of New York Mellon Corporation.

Boddy, David, Jane Dokko, Brad Hershbein, and Melissa S. Kearney, 2015. *Ten Economic Facts About Financial Well-Being in Retirement.* The Hamilton Project/The Brookings Institution.

Bodie, Zvi, Brett Hammond, and Olivia S. Mitchell, 2002. *A Framework for Analyzing and Managing Retirement Risks.* University of Pennsylvania Population Aging Research Center.

Bosworth, Barry P., Gary Burtless, and Mattan Alalouf, 2015. *Do Retired Americans Annuitize Too Little? Trends in the Share of Annuitized Income.* Boston College Center for Retirement Research.

Brady, Peter J., 2016. *How America Supports Retirement: Challenging the Conventional Wisdom on Who Benefits.* Washington, DC: Investment Company Institute.

Brady, Peter J., 2012. *The Tax Benefits and Revenue Costs of Tax Deferral.* Washington, DC: Investment Company Institute.

Brightscope and Investment Company Institute, 2014. *The Brightscope/ICI Defined Contribution Plan Profile: A Close Look at*

401(k) Plans. San Diego, CA: Brightscope and Washington, DC: Investment Company Institute.

Brown, Jeffrey R., and Scott J. Weisbenner, 2013. *Building Retirement Security Through Defined Contribution Plans.* University of Illinois at Urbana-Champaign.

Bubb, Ryan, Patrick Corrigan, and Patrick L. Warren, 2015. *A Behavioral Contract Theory Perspective on Retirement Savings.* New York University School of Law, Center for Law, Economics and Organization.

Butrica, Barbara A., and Nadia S. Karamcheva, 2015. *The Relationship Between Automatic Enrollment and DC Plan Contributions: Evidence from a National Survey of Older Workers.* Boston College Center for Retirement Research.

Callan Investment Institute, 2016. *2016 Defined Contribution Trends.* Callan Investment Institute.

Choi, James J., 2015. *Contributions to Defined Contribution Pension Plans.* National Bureau of Economic Research.

Choi, James J., David Laibson, and Brigitte C. Madrian, 2005. *$100 Dollar Bills on the Sidewalk: Suboptimal Savings in 401(k) Plans.* National Bureau of Economic Research.

Cerulli Associates, 2015. *Evolution of the Retirement Investor 2015: Insights into Investor Segmentation and the Retirement Income Landscape.* Cerulli Associates.

Citi, 2016. *The Coming Pension Crisis: Recommendations for Keeping the Global Pensions System Afloat.* Citi GPS: Global Perspectives & Solutions.

Collins, Sean, Sarah Holden, James Duvall, and Elena Barone Chism, 2016. *The Economics of Providing 401(k) Plans: Services, Fees and Expenses, 2015.* Investment Company Institute.

Davis, Rowland, and David Madland, 2013. *American Retirement Savings Could be Much Better.* Center for American Progress.

Defined Contribution Institutional Investment Association, 2015. *Retirement Income Solutions Guide for Plan Sponsors: Considerations and Case Studies to Help Employers Understand and*

Evaluate Retirement Income Options. Defined Contribution Institutional Investment Association.

Donaldson, Scott J., Francis M. Kinniry, Jr., Vytautas Maciulis, Andrew J. Patterson, and Michael A. DiJoseph, 2015. *Vanguard's Approach to Target-Date Funds.* Vanguard Research.

Edwards, Phil, Holly Donovan, and Chris Anast, 2015. *Defined Contribution Plan Success Factors: Framework for Plans with an Objective of Retirement Income Adequacy.* Defined Contribution Institutional Investment Association.

Ellis, Charles D., Alicia H. Munnell, and Andrew D. Eschtruth, 2014. *Falling Short: The Coming Retirement Crisis and What to Do About It.* New York, NY: Oxford University Press.

Ernst & Young, 2014. *Building a Better Retirement World: Insights for Better Outcomes in the Global Pension & Retirement Market.*

Friedman, John N., 2015. *Building on What Works: A Proposal to Modernize Retirement Savings.* The Hamilton Project/The Brookings Institution.

Gale, William G., J. Mark Iwry, David C. John, and Lina Walker, 2009. *Automatic: Changing the Way America Saves.* Washington, DC: Brookings Institution Press.

Gale, William G., Jonathan Gruber, and Peter R. Orszag, 2006. *Improving Opportunities and Incentives for Saving by Middle- and Low-Income Households.* The Hamilton Project/The Brookings Institution.

Gale, William G., J. Mark Iwry, and Peter R. Orszag, 2005. *The Saver's Credit: Expanding Retirement Savings for Middle- and Lower-Income Americans.* Retirement Security Project, Georgetown University Public Policy Institute and the Brookings Institution.

Georgetown University Center for Retirement Initiatives, 2016. *Comparison of Retirement Plan Design Features by State: California, Illinois, Oregon, Maryland and Connecticut.* Georgetown University McCourt School of Public Policy.

Georgetown University Law Center, 2010. *A Timeline of the Evolution of Retirement in the United States.*

Ghilarducci, Teresa, 2008. *When I'm Sixty-Four: The Plot Against Pensions and the Plan to Save Them.* Princeton, NJ: Princeton University Press.

Ghilarducci, Teresa, and Alex Pavlakis, 2016. *The States of Reform.* The New School, Schwartz Center for Economic Policy Analysis.

Ghilarducci, Teresa, and Christian E. Weller, 2015. *The Inefficiencies of Existing Retirement Savings Incentives.* The New School, Schwartz Center for Economic Policy Analysis.

Ghilarducci, Teresa, Zachary Knauss, and Bridget Fisher, 2015. *Now Is the Time to Add Retirement Accounts to Social Security: The Guaranteed Retirement Account Proposal.* The New School, Schwartz Center for Economic Policy Analysis.

Harris, Benjamin H., and Rachel M. Johnson, 2012. *Economic Effects of Automatic Enrollment in Individual Retirement Accounts.* AARP Public Policy Institute.

Helman, Ruth, Craig Copeland, and Jack Vanderhei, 2016. *The 2016 Retirement Confidence Survey: Work Confidence Stable, Retiree Confidence Continues to Increase.* Employee Benefit Research Institute (EBRI).

HSBC, 2013. *The Future of Retirement: A New Reality.* HSBC Retirement Holdings.

Inker, Ben, and Martin Tarlie, 2014. *Investing for Retirement: The Defined Contribution Challenge.*

Investment Company Institute, 2015. *The Federal Thrift Savings Plan: Can It be Duplicated?*

Investment Company Institute, 2015. *Retirement Plan Modernization Proposals.*

Investment Company Institute, 2013. *Our Strong Retirement System: An American Success Story.*

Investment Company Institute, 2012. *The Success of the U.S. Retirement System.*

Investment Company Institute, 2006. *401(k) Plans: A 25-Year Retrospective.*

Iyengar, Sheena S., Wei Jiang, and Gur Huberman, 2003. *How Much Choice Is Too Much? Contributions to 401(k) Retirement Plans.* Pension Research Council, Wharton School, University of Pennsylvania.

Jaconetti, Colleen M., Michael A. DiJoseph, Zoe B. Odenwalder, and Francis M. Kinniry, 2016. *From Assets to Income: A Goals-Based Approach to Retirement Spending.* Vanguard Research Paper.

John, David, and William G. Gale, 2015. *Structuring State Retirement Savings Plans: A Guide to Policy Design and Management Issues.* The Brookings Institution.

Kahn, Melissa, 2016. *Moving the Coverage Needle: Towards a National Framework to Address Retirement Access and Coverage.* State Street Global Advisors.

Kalamarides, John J., Robert J. Doyle, and Bennett Kleinbert, 2015. *Multiple Employer Plans: Expanding Retirement Savings Opportunities.* Prudential Financial.

Kalamarides, John J., and Srinivas D. Reddy, 2014. *Guaranteed Lifetime Income and the Importance of Plan Design.* Prudential Financial.

Katz, Lawrence F., and Alan B. Krueger, 2016. *The Rise and Nature of Alternative Work Arrangements in the United States, 1995-2015.* National Bureau of Economic Research.

Keim, Donald B., and Olivia S. Mitchell, 2015. *Simplifying Choices in Retirement Plan Design.* University of Pennsylvania, Wharton School, Pension Research Council.

Laursen, Eric, 2012. *The People's Pension: The Struggle to Defend Social Security Since Reagan.* Oakland, CA: AK Press.

Loewy, Daniel, Christopher Nikolich, and Vidya Rajappa, 2015. *Designing the Future of Target-Date Funds: A New Blueprint for Improving Retirement Outcomes.* Alliance Bernstein.

Lowenstein, Roger, 2008. *While America Aged: How Pension Debts Ruined General Motors, Stopped the NY Subways, Bankrupted*

San Diego and Loom as the Next Financial Crisis. New York, NY: The Penguin Press.

Lucas, Lori, and Maria Greindler, 2013. *Best Practices when Implementing Auto Features in DC Plans.* Defined Contribution Institutional Investment Association.

Lucas, Lori, Joshua Dietch, Suzanne V. Staveren, Catherine Peterson, Bridget Bearden, and Catherine Collinson, 2014. *Plan Sponsor Survey 2014: Focus on Automatic Plan Features.* Defined Contribution Institutional Investment Association.

Madland, David, Alex Rowell, and Rowland Davis, 2016. *Improving Americans' Retirement Outcomes Through the National Savings Plan.* Center for American Progress.

Madrian, Brigitte C., and Dennis F. Shea, 2001. "The Power of Suggestion: Inertia in 401(k) Participation and Savings Behavior". *Quarterly Journal of Economics.*

Mandell, Lewis, Pamela Perun, Lisa Mensah, and Raymond O'Mara, 2009. *Real Savings: An Automatic Investment Option for the Automatic IRA.* Aspen Institute Initiative on Financial Security.

Manyika, James, Susan Lund, Jacques Bughin, Kelsey Robinson, and Jan Mischke, 2016. *Independent Work: Choice, Necessity and the Gig Economy.* McKinsey Global Institute.

McGee, Josh B., 2015. *Defined Contribution Pensions Are Cost-Effective.* Manhattan Institute Center for State and Local Leadership.

McKinsey Global Institute, 2005. *The Graying of Europe: How Aging European Populations Will Threaten Living Standards and Prosperity.* McKinsey & Company.

McTigue, James R., and Charles A. Jeszeck, 2014. *Individual Retirement Accounts: Preliminary Information on IRA Balances Accumulated as of 2011.* U.S. Government Accountability Office.

Mensah, Lisa, Raymond O'Mara II, Colby Farber, and Robert Weinberger, 2012. *The Freedom Savings Credit: A Practical Step to Build Americans' Household Balance Sheets.* The Aspen Institute, Institute on Financial Security.

Miller, Judy A., 2014. *Retirement Savings for Low-Income Workers.* Testimony Submitted on Behalf of the American Society of Pension Professionals and Actuaries to the U.S. Senate Finance Committee Subcommittee on Social Security, Pensions and Family Policy.

Miller, Keith, David Madland, and Christian E. Weller, 2015. *The Reality of the Retirement Crisis.* Center for American Progress.

Mitchell, Olivia S., and Stephen P. Utkus, 2012. *Target Date Funds in 401(k) Retirement Plans.* National Bureau of Economic Research.

Mitchell, Olivia S., and Stephen P. Utkus, 2006. "How Behavioral Finance Can Inform Retirement Plan Design." *Journal of Applied Corporate Finance.*

Mitchell, Olivia S., and Stephen Utkus, 2004. *Pension Design and Structure, New Lessons from Behavioral Finance.* Pension Research Council Series, Oxford University Press.

Mitchell, Olivia S., and Stephen Utkus, 2003. *Lessons from Behavioral Finance for Retirement Plan Design.* University of Pennsylvania, Wharton School, Pension Research Council.

Morrissey, Monique, 2016. *The State of American Retirement: How 401(k)s Have Failed Most American Workers.* Economic Policy Institute.

Morse, David, 2014. *State Initiatives to Expand the Availability and Effectiveness of Private Sector Retirement Plans: How Federal Laws Apply to Plan Design Options.* Georgetown University, McCourt School of Public Policy Center for Retirement Initiatives.

Munnell, Alicia H., and Jean-Pierre Aubry, 2016. *The Funding of State and Local Pensions: 2015–2020.* Boston College Center for Retirement Research.

Munnell, Alicia H., and Jean-Pierre Aubry, 2016. *Will Pensions and OPEBs Break State and Local Budgets?* Boston College Center for Retirement Research.

Munnell, Alicia H., Jean-Pierre Aubry, and Caroline V. Crawford, 2016. *How Has the Shift to Defined Contribution Plans Affected Savings?* Boston College Center for Retirement Research.

Munnell, Alicia H., Anek Belbase, and Geoffrey T. Sanzenbacher, 2015. *State Initiatives to Cover Uncovered Private Sector Workers.* Boston College Center for Retirement Research.

Munnell, Alicia H., Matthew S. Rutledge, and Anthony Webb, 2015. *Are Retirees Falling Short? Reconciling the Conflicting Evidence.* Boston College Center for Retirement Research.

Munnell, Alicia H., Jean-Pierre Aubry, and Caroline V. Crawford, 2015. *Investment Returns: Defined Benefit vs. Defined Contribution Plans.* Boston College Center for Retirement Research.

Munnell, Alicia H, Jean-Pierre Aubry, and Mark Cafarelli, 2014. *Defined Contribution in the Public Sector: An Update.* Boston College Center for Retirement Research.

Munnell, Alicia H., 2014. *401(k)/IRA Holdings in 2013: An Update from the Federal Reserve Survey of Consumer Finances.* Boston College Center for Retirement Research.

Munnell, Alicia H., and Annika Sunden, 2004. *Coming Up Short: The Challenge of 401(k) Plans.* Washington, DC: Brookings Institution Press.

Natixis Global Asset Management, 2016. *Natixis Global Retirement Index.* Natixis Global Asset Management.

Northern Trust, 2016. *The Path Forward: Designing the Ideal Defined Contribution Plan.* Northern Trust.

Nybo, Stig, and Liz Alexander, 2013. *Transform Tomorrow: Awakening the Super Saver in Pursuit of Retirement Readiness.* Hoboken, NJ: John Wiley & Sons.

OECD, 2015. *Annual Survey of Large Pension Funds and Public Pension Reserve Funds: Report on Pension Funds' Long-Term*

Investments. Organization of Economic Cooperation and Development.

Oldroyd, Daniel, and Lynn Avitabile, 2015. *Off Balance: The Unintended Consequences of Prioritizing One Risk in Target Date Fund Design*. J.P. Morgan Asset Management.

Pew Charitable Trusts, 2016. *Employer-sponsored Retirement Plan Access, Uptake and Savings*. Pew Charitable Trusts.

Pew Charitable Trusts, 2016. *How States Are Working to Address the Retirement Savings Challenge: An Analysis of State-Sponsored Initiatives to Help Private Sector Workers Save*. Pew Charitable Trusts.

Pew Research Center, 2014. *Millennials in Adulthood: Detached from Institutions, Networked with Friends*. Pew Research Center.

Plan Sponsor Council of America, 2016. *59th Annual Survey: PSCA's Annual Survey of Profit Sharing and 401(k) Plans*.

Previtero, Alessandro, 2010. *Using Behavioral Finance to Help Employees Achieve their Retirement Saving Goals*. Standard Retirement Services.

Prudential, 2014. *Planning for Retirement: The Importance of Workplace Retirement Plans and Guaranteed Lifetime Income*. Prudential.

Purcell, Patrick, 2006. *Summary of the Pension Protection Act of 2006*. Congressional Research Service.

Reilly, Catherine, and Melissa Kahn, 2016. *Local Goals, Global Lessons: Building Retirement Security with Global Best Practices*. State Street Global Advisors.

Sanzenbacher, Geoffrey T., Anthony Webb, Natalia S. Orlova, and Candace M. Cosgrove, 2016. *Does a Uniform Retirement Age Make Sense?* Boston College, Center for Retirement Research.

Sass, Steven A., 2014. *The U.K.'s Ambitious New Retirement Savings Initiative*. Boston College Center for Retirement Research.

Schauss, Stacy L., William Allport, and Justin Blesy, 2013. *Global DC Plans: Similar Destinations, Distinctly Different Paths*. PIMCO.

Schieber, Sylvester J., 2012. *The Predictable Surprise: The Unraveling of the U.S. Retirement System*. New York, NY: Oxford University Press.

Scott, John, Andrew Blevins, Theron Guzoto, and Kevin Whitman, 2016. *Who's In, Who's Out: A Look at Access to Employer-Based Retirement Plans and Participation in the States*. Pew Charitable Trusts.

Sprague, Aleta, 2013. *The California Secure Choice Retirement Savings Program: An Innovative Response to the Coming Retirement Security Crisis*. New America Foundation.

T. Rowe Price, 2016. *The PPA 10 Years In: A Retirement Revolution Ready for Evolution*. Price Perspective, T. Rowe Price.

Thaler, Richard H., and Cass R. Sunstein, 2008. *Nudge: Improving Decisions About Health, Wealth and Happiness*. New Haven, CT: Yale University Press.

Thaler, Richard H., and Shlomo Benartzi, 2007. *The Behavioral Economics of Retirement Savings Behavior*. Washington DC: AARP Public Policy Group.

Thaler, Robert, and Shlomo Benartzi, 2004. "Save More Tomorrow: Using Behavioral Economics to Increase Employee Saving." *Journal of Political Economy*.

Towers Watson, 2012. *Today's Plan for Tomorrow's Retirees: Are We Building DC Plans That Measure Up?* Towers Watson.

Turner, John A., and Nari Rhee, 2013. *Lessons for Private Sector Retirement Security from Australia, Canada and the Netherlands*. National Institute on Retirement Security.

Transamerica, 2016. *The Current State of 401(k)s: The Employer's Perspective—16th Annual Transamerica Retirement Survey*. Transamerica Center for Retirement Studies.

Transamerica, 2015. *Prescience 2019: Expert Opinions on the Future of Retirement Plans*. Transamerica Retirement Solutions.

U.S. Government Accountability Office, 2016. *Retirement Security: Low Defined Contribution Savings May Pose Challenges.*

U.S. Government Accountability Office, 2016. *401(k) Plans: DOL Could Take Steps to Improve Income Options for Plan Participants.*

U.S. Government Accountability Office, 2015. *Retirement Security: Federal Action Could Help State Efforts to Expand Private Sector Coverage.*

U.S. Government Accountability Office, 2015. *Most Households Approaching Retirement Have Low Savings.*

U.S. Government Accountability Office, 2015. *401(k) Plans: Clearer Regulations Could Help Plan Sponsors Choose Investments for Participants.*

U.S. Government Accountability Office, 2015. *Contingent Workforce: Size, Characteristics, Earnings, and Benefits.*

U.S. Senate Committee on Finance, 2015. *The Savings & Investment Bipartisan Tax Working Group Report.* U.S. Senate.

VanDerhei, Jack, 2015. *How Does the Probability of a Successful Retirement Differ Between Participants in Final-Average Defined Benefit Plans and Voluntary Enrollment 401(k) Plans?* Employee Benefit Research Institute.

VanDerhei, Jack, 2015. *Auto-IRAs: How Much Would They Increase the Probability of Successful Retirements and Decrease Retirement Deficits? Preliminary Evidence from EBRI's Retirement Security Model.* Employee Benefit Research Institute.

VanDerhei, Jack, 2015. *Retirement Savings Shortfalls: Evidence from EBRI's Retirement Security Projection Model.* Employee Benefit Research Institute.

VanDerhei, Jack, 2014. *The Role of Social Security, Defined Benefits and Private Retirement Accounts in the Face of the Retirement Crisis.* Employee Benefit Research Institute.

VanDerhei, Jack, and Lori Lucas, 2010. *The Impact of Auto-Enrollment and Automatic Contribution Escalation on Retirement Income Adequacy.*

VanDerhei, Jack, and Craig Copeland, 2008. *The Impact of the PPA on Retirement Savings for 401(k) Participants*. Employee Benefit Research Institute.

VanDerhei, Jack, and Sarah Holden, 2005. *The Influence of Automatic Enrollment, Catch-Up and IRA Contributions on 401(k) Accumulations at Retirement*. Investment Company Institute.

Vanguard Research, 2016. *How America Saves 2016*. Vanguard Institutional Investor Group.

Willis Towers Watson, 2016. *Global Pensions Asset Study, 2016*.

Wolman, William, and Anne Colamosca, 2002. *The Great 401(k) Hoax: Why Your Family's Financial Security Is at Risk and What You Can Do About It*. Cambridge, MA: Basic Books.

Xanthopoulos, Judy, and Mary M. Schmitt, 2012. *Retirement Savings and Tax Expenditure Estimates*. American Society of Pension Professionals & Actuaries (ASPPA).

Young, Jean A., 2015. *The Auto Savings Generation: Steering Millennials to Better Retirement Outcomes*. Vanguard Center for Retirement Research.

Zelinsky, Edward A., 2007. *Origins of the Ownership Society: How the Defined Contribution Paradigm Changed America*, New York, NY: Oxford University Press.

INDEX

ABOUT THE AUTHORS

Robert L. Reynolds is the President and CEO of Putnam Investments and Great-West Financial, which includes
Empower Retirement, the nation's second-largest provider
of retirement services to over 8 million retirement savers. His
career in investments and retirement services dates back to the
mid-1980s when he took charge of Fidelity's then-small 401(k)
business and grew it more than 100-fold—from $3 billion to
over $300 billion by the year 2000 when he stepped up to the
role of Vice Chairman and Chief Operating Officer of Fidelity
Investments.

Reynolds was a hands-on pioneer in developing 401(k) plans
into the prime source of working Americans' future retirement
income. He either led or adopted early a host of innovations in
workplace savings ranging from daily pricing of savers' assets to
the use of target date funds as "default" investments for those
who make no choice on their own. He has earned multiple
industry leadership awards, including Retirement Leader of
the Year and *Plan Sponsor* Magazine's Lifetime Achievement
Award for his role in building up the 401(k) savings system.

Actively engaged in public policy debate and advocacy for
decades, Reynolds played an important role in backing Speaker
John Boehner's efforts to pass the landmark Pension Protection
Act of 2006. He frequently meets with leading members of
the House of Representatives and the Senate and has testified
extensively before Congress on retirement policy issues.

A proud son of West Virginia and a graduate of West Virginia University, Reynolds supports multiple charities and boards including the Massachusetts General Hospital's President's Council, the Boys and Girls Clubs of Greater Boston, The American Ireland Fund, the Dana-Farber Cancer Institute, and West Virginia University. An avid skier, he is on the board of the U.S. Ski and Snowboard Association and is a passionate fan of the New England Patriots and the Boston Red Sox and Celtics. Mr. Reynolds and his wife, Laura, live in Concord, Massachusetts, close by the site of the first American victory in the Revolutionary War. "Just being there," he says, "reminds me to always bet on America."

Lenny Glynn is Director of Public Policy for Putnam Investments and Empower Retirement. His career in journalism included stints at *TIME*, *Newsweek*, *Businessweek*, and *Institutional Investor* magazines and articles for the *New York Times*, *Vogue*, and many other publications. He served as a speechwriter in the presidential campaigns of Michael Dukakis in 1988 and Bill Clinton in 1992 and as head speechwriter for the U.S. Department of Transportation. Since 1995, he has held top executive communication and policy posts for State Street Corporation and Fidelity Investments before joining Putnam Investments in 2008.

John Mitchem, Head of JM3 Projects, has worked in journalism, public policy, executive communications, and content marketing since the 1970s. His focus has been on emerging technologies, economic development, global capital markets, and innovations in healthcare, education, and retirement finance.

After over two decades with the United Nations and the State Street Corporation, he founded his firm, JM3 Projects, which has done thought leadership projects with a variety of major financial companies and trade associations as well as with government agencies, universities, and nongovernmental organizations around the world.